MW01602485

Rehearsing the Truth

...and He called Himself, "I AM"

[handwritten inscription:] The Great "I Am" is with you – May everyday bring a "desire" to "know Him more"

Lisa A. Mars,

God Bless You.

Lisa Mars :)

ISBN: 9798642751480
Lisa A. Mars * 10-14-1962 ~

I dedicate this book to the Memory of my Son, whom without, none of this would have come to be~

I love you Son!

Jacob Gerald Mars

3-12-88 ~ 2-11-04

Safe in the arms of Jesus!

Thank you Papa God for all those you've sent my way who have encouraged and cheered me on, ~ you know who you are, thank you!

I would also like to thank Linda Ryan for her undying love for me in teaching me the principles that lie within the text of this book.

I'd like to acknowledge Dan & Joe, who encouraged me greatly in the writing and titling of this work.

To the men and women of God who guided and encouraged me through publishing this work.

Last, but not least, thank you Duane for supporting me in all my endeavors.

Statement of Faith

I believe in the one true God
manifesting in three persons

God the Father
God the Son
God the Holy Spirit

I believe in life everlasting

I believe Jesus was crucified

I believe Jesus rose again for mankind's sin

I believe that we who believe will rise again
and be with him forever in eternity

I believe that salvation is by grace,
it's a free gift from God

I believe in the baptism of the Holy Spirit

I believe that the word of God~
the bible, is without error

I believe God desires that no one should
perish, he also desires that all people would
come to the saving knowledge and grace of the
Lord Jesus Christ~ who is the great "I AM"

And God said to Moses, *I AM THAT I AM* ~

and he said, thus shall

you say to the children of Israel,

***I AM* has sent me to you.**

Exodus 3:14, 15c

This is my name forever,

this is my memorial-name to all generations.

The following article is by *C. Kingsley* ~ He explains *"I AM"* way better than I.

If I say "*I am*," I say what is not true of me. I must say "I am something ~ I'm a man, I'm bad, I'm good, or I'm an Englishman, I'm a soldier, I'm a sailor, I'm a pastor." ~ and then I shall say what is true of me. Only God alone can say "I AM" without saying anything more. Why?, because God alone "is". Everybody and everything else in the world becomes: but God "is". We are all becoming something from our birth to our death ~ changing continually and becoming something different from what we were a minute before. First of all, we were created and made, and so became man. Since then we have been every moment changing~ becoming older, wiser, or alas~ foolisher, becoming stronger or weaker, becoming better or worse. Even our bodies are changing and becoming different day by day. God however, never ever changes or becomes anything different from what he is now, what he is, that he was~ and forever will be.

Many heathen men have known that there was one eternal God and that God is. They did not know that God Himself had said I AM, because of this they were made anxious, puzzled, almost desperate, so that the wiser they were, the unhappier they were. For what use is it merely knowing that God is? The question for poor human creatures is, "But what sort of a being is God?' Is He far off? Does He care nothing about us? Does He let the world go its own way, right or wrong? Is He proud and careless? A self-glorifying deity whose mercy is not over all His works, or even over any of them? And the glory of the Bible, the power of God revealed in the Bible is, that it answers the question and says, "God does care for men, God does see men, God is not far off from any one of us. God in sundry times and diverse manners spoke to our fathers by the prophets and said, "I AM." Moses said, "I AM" hath sent me." God does not merely love us and leave us to ourselves. He sends after us. He sends to us. But again: "I AM" hath sent me unto you." Unto whom? Who was Moses sent to? To the Children of Israel in Egypt. And what sort of people were they? Were they wise and learned? On the contrary, they were stupid, ignorant and brutish. Were they pious and godly? On the contrary, they were worshipping the foolish idols of the Egyptians ~ so fond of idolatry that they made a golden calf and worshiped it. Then why did God take such trouble for them? Why did God care for them, help them and work wonders for them? Why did he? It was precisely because they were so bad and just because they were so bad, His goodness yearned over them all the more and longed to make them good. Just because they were so unclean and brutish, his holiness longed all the more to cleanse them. Because they were so stupid and ignorant, his wisdom longed to make them wise. Because they were so miserable, his pity yearned over them, as a father over a child fallen into danger. Because they were sick, they had all the more need of a physician. Because they were lost, there was all the more reason for seeking and saving them. Because they were utterly weak, God desired all the more to put his strength into them~ so that his strength might be made perfect in weakness. Amen!

Introduction

If we desire to live an abundant life we must learn to rely on the words of God. The promises found in the bible are seeds of the faith, hope and love that we all need. God's word is not only the seed we need, it's also the water and the fertilizer which is necessary to sprout and grow us into fully mature, faithful and fruitful followers of Christ. God's promises are not an optional sometimes blessing to enhance our lives occasionally, rather his word is a means by which to change our lives for the good permanently. His promises are true, his word will be the bridge that transports us from the bondage and despair of our old lives into the hope and freedom that's found in and through the Lord Jesus Christ as we start our new life in him.

His divine power has given us everything we need for a godly life through our knowledge of him who called us by his own glory and goodness. Through these he has given us his _very_ _great_ _and_ _precious_ _promises,_ so that through them you may participate in the divine nature, having escaped the corruption in the world caused by evil desires. 2 Peter 1:3-4

This same verse in another version says~ _precious and magnificent promises,_ isn't this what we all desire? His very great, precious and magnificent promises! Ohh, "to know him more"!

When we fill our minds with the word of God, it's then that the word of God will renew our minds, then when this renewing of the mind happens, his very great and precious promises will become realized in our lives. I'm not really sure *how* it happens, all I know is *that* it happens! Friends, when we do this, (fill our minds with his word) we really have all that we need~ because all that we need is him!

According to Ephesians 1:17-18 to *"know him more"* is the objective of our faith, I pray this for you now, that you may know him more and more and more and more! It is the Lord's promises that empower us to overcome each trial no matter how fiery they may be. Along with every temptation we face and every single lie that the enemy of our souls will ever tempt us with, God's word will enable us to withstand, endure and overcome.

I'm saying this~ that with Gods word and the promises therein, every day we can start at the place of victory and every day we can end at the same place, that place is victory my friends!. Hallelujah! Let me repeat this, *every day* as believers when we choose to start at the place of victory, every day we'll end at the place of victory!

It is our own thinking that will determine how we relate to any and everyone. Our thinking impacts how we view ourselves, others, our marriages, our children and it impacts our relationship with God as well. In order to improve these relationships we must take our fallen faulty thinking and conform it to biblical standards. Years ago I asked a mentor how to deal with an unacceptable behavior, (in someone else) that was just so wrong (from my vantage point). I can recall her saying that it was simple, (I needed simple so I was very eager for her reply). Then she said, all I had to do was~ change my mind! I recall the scream inside of me saying, and just how do I do that!? Arggggg~

I was not pleased with her response, however, it's often only in hindsight that we're able to see the value and wisdom in that advice. In other words, we *get to* change our minds and line it up with what the bible says~ for this is truly where our victory begins! The very first step in changing our minds is to humble ourselves by admitting we don't know it all and the next step is to begin to read our bible to find out what pleases God.

When we discover our faulty thinking it will be our responsibility and privilege to conform ourselves to what his word says we are. Simply by admitting we've been wrong, asking for and receiving his forgiveness and determining in our hearts that we will continue to walk in the truth, we will thereby be changing our minds as we line up our thoughts with what the bible says is true. This is a lifetime process and does not come without many challenges.

Galatians 6:9 encourages us in this way: **Do not grow weary in well doing for we will surely reap a harvest if we do not give up!**

So let's not give up so easily my friends, let's continue to renew our minds day by day as we get into his word, thereby we will be training ourselves to walk in his righteousness daily!

Do not conform to the pattern of this world, but be transformed by the renewing of your mind. Then you will be able to test and approve what God's will is- his good, pleasing and perfect will. Romans 12:2

If the above verse says that we are to renew our minds, (and it does), then it must be totally possible to do so. The following are some quotes that lead us to believe and confirm what we already know to be the truth concerning our thoughts and how they become the leaders in our lives.

Your beliefs become your thoughts, your thoughts become your words, your words become your actions, your actions become your habits, your habits become your values and your values become your destiny.
~ *Mahatma Ghandi*

It is only by taking the fact of eternity into account that we can deliver thought from its slavery of life. And it is only by deliberately paying our attention and our primary allegiance to eternity that we can prevent time from turning our lives into a pointless or diabolical foolery.
~ *Aldous Huxley*

The whole function of thought is to produce habits of action.
~ *Charles S. Pierce*

Do you not see how necessary a world of pains and troubles is to school an intelligence and make it a soul? ~ *John Keats*

Knowledge, attitude and skills - hence your lifestyle - are driven and controlled by your thinking. ~ *Dr. Caroline Leaf*

The only place where your dream becomes impossible is in your own thinking. ~ *Robert H Schuller*

All you can do is change yourself and sometimes that changes everything! ~ *Gary W. Goldstein*

If you can change your mind, you can change your life. ~ *William James*

If you think you can or you think you can't ~ you're right. ~ *Henry Ford*

When people will not weed their own minds, they are apt to be overrun by nettles. ~ *Horace Walpole*

The world as we have created it is a process of our thinking. It cannot be changed without changing our thinking. ~ *Albert Einstein*

If we would only realize how powerful our thoughts really are, we would never, ever, ever again think to think a negative thought!

But the natural man does not receive the things of the Spirit of God, for they are foolishness to him. 1 Corinthians 2:14

The problem for some is that God's word often offends our natural minds. Let's consider the biblical ideas of submission or forgiveness. These things do not come easy to us because of our sinful state. The world and those in it according to Isaiah 55:8 simply do not think the way God does, for his way of thinking is much higher than ours.

Parenting a toddler can reflect this reality. You can not reason with a two-year-old about the necessity of picking up their toys because it's bedtime. They're just not capable of thinking the way adults do. A parent knows it's late and that if the little one doesn't get a full night of sleep, tomorrow may not be a happy day.

Foolishness is bound up in the heart of a child, but the rod of discipline will remove it far from him. Proverbs 22:15

The rod spoken of here is the rod that was used by shepherds to beat off the enemy, (the enemy spoken of here would have been the wolves who killed and ate the sheep) the rod was never used to strike the sheep.

Foolishness in this verse has the connotation of being thoughtless or being without understanding. So, we must realize that the rod we use today is really a metaphor. Spiritually speaking, our tongue and intellect is intended to be used as the tool of discipline to beat off the enemy of foolishness, which may simply be ignorance that a child may be displaying, rather than using a belt, wooden spoon or a hand.

What this means is that we need to educate our children's minds and beat off the enemy, which depending upon the age of the child, may be rebellion or could it simply be ignorance on the child's part because they have not yet learned or been taught. This verse is often misunderstood, even by the church to be literal spanking. On the contrary, it (spanking) may cause the anger, wounded-ness and or the rebellion. This is just one example, so let's look at another verse. **But I say unto you, Love your enemies, bless them that curse you, do good to them that hate you and pray for them which despitefully use you and persecute you.** Matthew 5:44

The bible tells us to love our enemies, but, just how in the heck do we do that? How do we bless those who persecute us? Do good to those who hate us? No, no, no... we want to give it right back to them! In our minds we say that they don't deserve a blessing after what they did. They owe me, they deserve to be punished, gosh darn it!

Sometimes the commands in scripture are offensive to us, however, we know they come from our loving Heavenly Father who knows what's best. So, will I live according to my limited understanding or will I choose to trust my Father in heaven who truly knows best?

The word of God often requires us to act contrary to our feelings. Often we may treat each other poorly because were living in fear. We hear the voice say "if I do that they'll just walk all over me" or "somebody has to teach them a lesson". The reason we don't think it will work is because we have misplaced faith and believe the voice in our own heads more that what God's word says. It is vital for us to learn how to trust God's plan. With growing faith, we can begin to believe what God says. We can treat each other the way God says to despite what our feelings may be dictating to us~ and in the end we may just end up saving our relationships. The word of God will not cater to our feelings; actually his word should and will challenge us. When we choose to honor God and his word, his word will also bring healing. Then and only then will our fears be transformed into faith!

Often times the word of God contradicts what we believe is true. These may be deeply held beliefs. For instance, the Pharisees knew the Torah, the first five books of the Bible. They memorized it and quoted it all the time. But Jesus told them, **"If you abide in my word, you are my disciples indeed"** John 8:31.

This shocked the Pharisees. They thought no one was more familiar with the Torah than them. If anyone was "abiding" in Scripture already, it was the Pharisees. Who was Jesus to tell them they needed more of the word? They didn't understand. They were mean-spirited. They lacked love. Jesus told them that although they may know the Bible, their lack of love indicated they didn't understand the Truth.

These are challenges to changing our minds. In order to let God's word change our mind, we have to have a teachable spirit. I and countless others have been transformed by the word of God because we sit at his feet, asking him to teach us. I confess that I am not perfect, but~ Jesus thinks I'm to die for! I have changed in many ways and the more I know, the more I need to know. Ahhh, *"to know him more"*, this is what it's all about!

As you *abide* (dwell in, take up residence in) in his word and *commit to it* as the standard of truth in your life, his word will transform your thinking and therefore your life. I may truly say to the Lord that: **I have hidden your word in my heart that I might not sin against you.** Psalm 119:11 ~ As you proceed to read, may you be found to hide his word in your heart as well! What are you waiting for… let's jump right in and may the word of God come alive on the inside of you as you do! I pray you will be blessed, be challenged and grow as I introduce myself to you in the following pages and as you begin or continue your own personal journey to "know him more". As I worked on this writing in 2014 I was a frequent shopper at my local ALDI'S store where Joe, (the manager) and I would have small talk. I shared with him that I was writing a book, he asked me what the title of it was, (at which time I hadn't yet seriously considered a title). Joe made a comment about what Father God called himself, and the moment it came out of his mouth, I knew that it would be the title of this book. Thank you Joe for the inspiration, May God bless you richly for your kindness and contribution!

Little did I know that *Almighty God* would show up at my local ALDI store to give me the title to the book you now hold in your hands! I have learned that *"to know him more"* means he will deliver what I need exactly when and where I need it! Hallelujah!!!

...and He called himself "I AM"

Rehearsing the Truth

And God said to Moses, *I AM THAT I AM*~ and he said, Thus shall you say to the children of Israel, *I AM* has sent me to you. Exodus 3:14

This whole "*I am*" journey started for me many years ago and it's here in these pages that I would love to share with you, the reader, my story. Lil, who is an older friend of mine, called to invite me to a Bible Study Fellowship (B.S.F.) meeting, which is an internationally known bible study group. I had an appointment with the funeral home that particular morning so I declined the invitation saying maybe another time. The reason I declined is because I was trying to regain some sense of direction after my youngest son Jake's death. He had been diagnosed with Leukemia on April 21, 2003, he underwent a bone marrow transplant three months later and on February 11, 2004 Jake moved in with Jesus~ just a month shy of his sixteenth birthday.

It was just a couple of weeks after Jake moved out of the house and in with Jesus that I was walking and praying in my neighborhood. It was Spring and needless to say, I was feeling very lost *and* alone. Duane, my husband of 25 years, had changed jobs the week after Jake died and by now our marriage had been dead, d-e-a-d for a long time, so I was telling him (God) I was going to be a Mom for a couple of more years. It was then that I asked him, "What am I supposed to do now?" I felt like I had been fired from my job ~ if you've ever been fired, you know what I'm talking about, I felt devastated. As I continued walking I asked the Lord, (rather tersely at that), "So, what is my job description now?" ~ Immediately I heard God's still small voice say, "*to know me more*".

Wowza, was I thrilled, my heart leapt with joy because I had just been given a new job description! Though I had no idea what "*to know him more*" might involve, I was excited because I suddenly had a purpose and a reason to get up in the morning! The major responsibilities in my life were non-existent, my older sons Josh and Jesse were already living away from home by this time and Jake was with Jesus so the daily trips to the hospital and the barista job I had quit to take care of him were absent. Duane had just started a new job so all of his energies were focused on that. Since it was just springtime, gardening was not going to be a distraction, not for a while anyway.

As you can see there was nothing standing in my way and with no outside commitments I had all the time in the world that one would need "*to know him more*". When Linda called inviting me to a B.S.F. meeting for the following morning I understood that it was the Lord who was prompting and inviting me to go and much to Linda's surprise I told her I'd change the appointment at the funeral home and that I would see her there in the morning. Incidentally, this was the very same meeting that Lil had also invited me to.

Since this was the beginning of the beginning of the *"I Am"* story, I'd like to share with you when, where and how I first met Linda. I started attending at Grace United Methodist Church in North Minneapolis, Minnesota in September of 1997. I was born again the third of December that same year, while Jake was born again a couple of months before me so we attended church together, he was nine and I was thirty-five. This congregation only had about thirty members so there was a great need for teachers. Although Linda didn't attend services there, it didn't take me long to realize what Linda was doing. She attended the early service at her home church then she would scoot over to our church to teach, one of her students was my Jacob. I was so impressed that she would commit to this small little church and give her time so freely. There was definitely something different about her, I could see her enthusiasm along with her passion for the kids and though I never conversed with her, I admired her greatly. We continued to attend Grace for about a year and a half even after we moved to Blaine. It was several years later through a mutual friend that I heard Linda was still involved with the kids at Grace Church.

Fast forward to 2003 when Jake was diagnosed (six years had passed since we met Linda), he asked me to call her to see if she would come and pray for him. Linda eagerly accepted the invitation and was delighted that Jake would not only remember her, but that he would ask her to come and pray with him. When Linda arrived at our home Jake was lying on the couch not feeling so well. Linda sat down next to him and began to testify to us of the recent miracles she witnessed on a missions trip, (she had just arrived home from Africa) she shared other testimonies of healing and even of raising the dead, Jake was very encouraged in his faith, as was I.

Linda then prayed for Jake and although he was not instantly healed of the cancer the Lord miraculously healed him in some other ways. Though greatly encouraged but ignorant of God's will concerning healing we continued on with the prescribed medical treatments including chemotherapy, radiation and a bone marrow transplant.

During the ten months from diagnosis to death I spoke many words of life and health over Jake. As we prayed and read scripture together daily we became very close. Jake would be in the hospital more than he'd be at home during this time so he wanted an audio bible along with a CD player for his hospital room, so we made the purchase for him (with his money) and brought it to him right away. He wanted to have the scriptures softly playing in his room whether he had visitors or not and especially overnight as he slept. Having the scriptures pouring forth over him like this brought Jake (and me) great comfort. Though it may not have been as comforting as having Mom right there, it had a way of changing the atmosphere in his room, it brought peace despite the chaos. Before Jake was diagnosed he was testing the things of the world and had been growing distant from God. As his Mom I was grateful to see that he once again desired the things of the Lord, he was reaching for and clinging to our heavenly Father. This was and is a wonderful testimony of how faithful God is, even and especially in our wanderings.

It was in one of the many hospital rooms Jake had that a verse of scripture came alive for me. It was James 1:2 ~ **Consider it pure joy my brethren when you face trials of many kinds.** It was about midnight and I was totally helpless to relieve the pain Jake's body was in. I turned to the scriptures and started to read them aloud to him. I read and read and I read some more until his symptoms subsided and he was finally asleep. My heart still aches a bit thinking of that time, yet I rejoice because I grew stronger in my faith as I sat on that window bench reading God's word with the light that was streaming in through the blinds from the hallway. Once Jake was sound asleep I continued reading the scriptures until I too was at peace, knowing I was safe in my Fathers care, I too drifted off to sleep. What I learned from this situation is that it is from these trials that God reveals to me what is really in my heart: Will I turn to him in my time of need and fully rely on him and his word to sustain me, or, will I in my own self effort fail to find the peace that comes from abiding and persevering in his love.

It was about six months after Linda's first visit with Jake that she was attending a Curves location near her home. Linda was speaking with Liz, an employee there as well as a prayer partner. Liz was requesting prayer for a family in her congregation whose fifteen year old son had just passed away after battling Leukemia. Though they prayed together often and shared requests Linda was shocked to discover that it was our beloved Jake and his family that Liz was requesting prayer for that day. Though I did not know Liz personally, her granddaughter was in youth group with Jake at the church we both attended at the time. What a mighty God we serve, I was so blessed to discover and meet some of the great women of faith who had been praying for me and my family.

Through Linda's obedience to serve as a missionary Sunday school teacher, in answering a fifteen year old boys request for prayer six years later, our Father in heaven who knows it all made sure Linda would hear about Jakes death, attend his funeral and then prompt her to call me with an invitation to a B.S.F. meeting just three weeks after his death ~ no one but the Great "I AM" could have put all these details together and this is the God I call Father.

Back to the B.S.F. meeting, Father was already beginning to reveal to me who he was. He knew what I was going through and so he placed me in a group whose leader personally knew how to help me go through this fiery trial. What I soon discovered about the leader is that she too had experienced the death of a child. *Selah!* Let me ask you a question ~ Do you think that it was just a mere coincidence that out of thirty plus groups of women, I just happened to end up in hers? ~ I think not! Without saying a word she understood it all and God in his infinite wisdom, the one who sees it all and who knows it all provided just what I needed during this time in my life. Experiencing his compassion for me in this way, only led me *"to know him more"*.

When I started attending B.S.F. in March of 2004 there were about ten weeks left before the summer break. One day in April Linda saw me after class and asked me how my prayer life was going. Unbeknownst to me, years earlier she had observed me while at Grace Church and saw that I had a true heart of worship and in light of the circumstances she was concerned about me. I replied that my prayer life was ehh, you know, not so much (grief and shock can do strange things to the mind and body). Although Linda and I were mere acquaintances she invited me to her home so that we might pray together. Though I had admired her previously I was not exactly excited about the prospect of driving all the way to Brooklyn Center (about 10 miles) to a near strangers home to pray and suggested we pray over the phone. Linda stated we could do it that way, however it would be harder to enter into the presence of the Lord that way. That made sense so we set a time for the following Tuesday to meet at her home. When I arrived at her home I sat down on the couch while Linda put on a worship CD. For the next hour or so we sang and worshipped and when the music ended we prayed together for a while.

When our time was over I hugged her and asked "so when could we do this again?!" Secretly she hoped we would meet regularly, so of course she was delighted when I asked and with that we began meeting weekly for worship and prayer. So, this is how God brought Linda and I together, little did I know then what God had in store for the two of us going forward. Some years later Linda shared with me how reluctant she was to call and invite me to B.S.F. thinking that she herself would have to convince me to attend. She was blown away that I so readily accepted the invitation and only later realized that the Holy Spirit had already prepared me for such a time as this.

Once again, the Great "*I Am*" had provided for my needs, I needed grounding and I needed some sort of a regimen, something that would help to keep me on track and this was it. That day worshipping at Linda's home the embers burning inside of me were fanned into flames, I felt alive again! Not only did the Lord bring Linda into my everyday life at that time, he also brought some other great women into my life as well, they all offered support and encouragement in the midst of the storm.

My pastor's wife faithfully met with me weekly for conversation and prayer those first months after Jake's home-going. My neighbors were wonderful. Before, during and after Jakes treatments. the lawn was mowed, meals were brought, our home cleaned! Then there were also other women at my church who supported me through prayer, cards and encouragement and of course there was love me up Lil! My Lil, was and is a very special friend who prayed and prayed and prayed and is still praying for me and my family to this day ten years later, as I am writing this. Jake would always affectionately refer to her as Grandma Lil ~ A simple thank-you Father would definitely be an understatement for the gift of these women in my life during this time. I was discovering that *"to know him more"* meant he'd always provide friendship, fellowship and encouragement~ not only to get us through the hard times, but to get us through in all times.

I became eager to worship and pray with Linda so Tuesday's became the highlight of my week. At some point Linda mentioned something about doing a six week video Healing School and wondered if I might be interested in attending, I told her I definitely would. It wasn't long after that when Linda started the School, take a guess who one of the other attendees was, it was the prayer partner and employee from Curves, none other than Liz herself~ *oh "to know him more"*~ isn't my Daddy wonderful! When I think about this I am in *awe* of the Father's graciousness and outpouring of love, aren't you! *Selah!*

Although I came to know Jesus as my personal Savior seven years previous it was during this six week Healing School that I discovered much more about God and his redemptive plan for me! I learned that salvation included a lot more than just going to heaven when I die.

In the following paragraph you will see the excerpt from the *Greater Works Ministries* teaching we created titled *"The Whole Gospel"* that I first learned and subsequently have taught many others as well, I trust you also will be encouraged. It was through the Healing School that I discovered my heavenly Father to be my *deliverer*, my *healer*, my *protector*, my *defender*, my *provider* and *a whole lot more*! I pray you too will discover him in these ways! Amen and Amen!

The Whole Gospel

"The word is near you; it is in your mouth and in your heart, that is, the word of faith we are proclaiming: That if you confess with your mouth, "Jesus is Lord," and believe in your heart that God raised him from the dead, you will be saved*. *(delivered, protected, healed, preserved, be blessed to do well and be made whole)* **For it is with your heart that you believe and are justified, and it is with your mouth that you confess and are saved.** *(delivered, protected, healed, preserved, be blessed to do well and be made whole)* **As the Scripture says, "Anyone who trusts in him will never be put to shame." For there is no difference between Jew and Gentile— the same Lord is Lord of all and richly blesses all who call on him, for "Everyone who calls on the name of the Lord will be saved."** *(delivered, protected, healed, preserved, be blessed to do well and be made whole)* Romans 10:8-13

*Strong's Concordance G.4982 saved, sozo-
to save, deliver, protect, heal, preserve, do well, be made whole
(same root word as soteria- G.4991, rescue, safety, deliverance, health, salvation)

Attending the Healing School was a huge step to understanding and *"knowing him more"*. At the end of the course Linda commented that she was not sure if she would do this again (hold a healing school that is) and I very quickly said, *Oh* yes you are! I am not sure where it came from at the time, but it flew out of my mouth as if a bird in flight.

When Linda and I met the following morning for worship and prayer she reminded me of what I had said and then added this, "you're right in saying I will do this again and you'll be teaching the second weeks class because I'll be out of town!" (*gasp! gasp! gasp!*) Little did I know the day before that I was prophetically speaking. (I didn't even know what that meant!) What was about to be revealed to me is that the Lord had conceived Greater Works Ministries months and years earlier in Linda's heart and now it was about to be birthed. Over the next four years we went on to hold sixteen schools together before Linda and her husband Bob developed the Healing School on-line as the Lord led me in a different direction. According to Jeremiah 29:11 *"knowing him more"* meant learning that his plans and purposes for our lives have been planned before we even were. He lovingly reveals his plan to us as we seek to "know him more". His plans and purposes will prevail despite the hardships, I now know *for sure* that what the enemy has meant for evil, God uses for our good. Amen

If you are interested in some more great teachings from the Healing School of Greater Works Ministries feel free to check it out on-line.

There you will find many testimonies of students including one from Ruth T., (that's my Mom) which I must share with you. My parents were visiting (from Texas) that summer for a family wedding when the Holy Spirit impressed it upon my heart to invite them to the Healing School starting the same evening they were arriving. They had just driven for two days to get here so I looked for every excuse not to invite them because it was I who was afraid. During the seven mile drive to the meeting place the Holy Spirit's prompting would not let me alone so when I arrived at the building I did call (my own house where they were staying) to invite them. Though my Dad didn't attend that evening, my Mom did and to *this day* I praise God for prompting me to invite them because he not only healed my Mom that evening, he saved her as well! All she could say was thank you Jesus, thank you Jesus! It was the first time I ever saw tears in my Mom's eyes, it was a glorious evening. Hallelujah, Praise the Lord, He is mighty to save!

Father taught me about Isaiah 50:2b that night. I now know that his hand is not so short that it cannot save, he did and he does! That was over a decade ago and during this time I have watched Father God use my Mom in mighty ways in her little hometown of Ingram, Texas. To this day she regularly lays hands on the sick and sees them recover! I not only call her Mom, I call her Sister, Daughter and Friend! What an amazing God we serve! You can find her personal testimony on-line or in the index at the back of the book.

Thank you Jesus!   You are mighty to SAVE!   Hallelujah!

I could not have known any of this would transpire when Linda first came to that small little church in North Minneapolis to teach Sunday school. Remembering and writing these ten years later I am in *awe* of how my gracious heavenly Father accomplishes his plans and purposes in the most unusual of ways. In the intervening years he has continued to reveal himself, his love and his character to me. Little did I know when I demanded to know what my job description, that *"to know him more"* would become a lifelong journey. (As of 2018 when I am currently finishing this work, it has been 14 years since the Lord gave me this job description, *"to know him more"*, some days I shine and some days I shine brighter! Hallelujah!)

For I know the plans I have for you (Lisa) **declares the LORD. Plans to prosper you and not to harm you, plans to give you a hope and a future.** Jeremiah 29:11 ~

Stranger things have happened and what follows is a testimony of how good things can be brought out of difficult circumstances. At Jakes funeral, Josh who is now thirty-three was re-introduced to Chelsea who had a crush on him in High School. Josh's best buddy at that time was Nate, Chelsea is Nate's cousin. Though there had been no contact for the intervening years, Heidi, (Nate's sister) upon hearing of Jakes death called Chelsea and insisted that they attend Jakes funeral together so they could see Josh. So when the kids ask how Daddy met Mommy, Josh can tell them, she was my buddy Nate's little cousin and she was at his house all the time when I was over there. She had a crush on me but I was too old for her at the time and I was heading off to the army after I graduated anyway. Six years later when your Mom showed up at your Uncle Jake's funeral I was quite surprised. We starting dating after that, I proposed to her sixteen months later, and then we were married July 1, 2006 in a beautiful outdoor ceremony. I include this to share with you the reader, that even out of the seeming darkness God gives us good gifts as James 1:17 describes. Josh and Chelsea have been married many years now and are currently residing in Plymouth, Minnesota.

It was through Nate, Josh's buddy from High School and a flyer from my A.A. group that I was first invited to attend the little North Minneapolis Church where I was saved and then introduced to Linda. Father had plans all along to bring Linda and I together to co-found Greater Works Ministries, a ministry that would see hundreds delivered, healed, filled, preserved, blessed to do well and be made whole, including me! Earlier I mentioned that Linda continued to work with the children's ministry for several years after my family moved to Blaine. It was with Nate, (Josh's buddy) that Linda was doing the children's ministry with. So funny! Isn't it amazing how he brings people and circumstances together, I am in AWE, aren't you!

Let's get back to the *"I Am"* journey. It was early in 2005 that we held the second Greater Works Ministries Healing School that I, Lisa, would co-teach. Although there were just three students attending, this is where the Lord taught me about Zachariah 4:10. This verse teaches us that we are not to despise the day of small beginnings, we didn't and our class size grew!

It continues to amaze me how God uses the foolish things of the world to confound the wise and how he blesses those of us who are hungry for his truth and who are willing to step out in obedience so that others may also *"know him more"*. That's my Daddy, it's just the way he is and that's *"AWESOME"*, wouldn't you agree?

About a year later as we continued to meet weekly for praise, prayer and planning I was speaking about some symptoms in my body and Linda asked me this very important question (this whole book is predicated upon it) that has changed and transformed my life and if you will let it, it will transform and change your life as well. She simply asked me this, and I quote, *"What scripture are you standing on?"* I had heard this terminology around the church, however I really had no clue as to what it meant, so Linda carefully and simply explained it to me.

She encouraged me to put together some scriptures that spoke to the issues I was facing and then to "stand on them", meaning I was to begin speaking them over myself (yes, out loud) calling those things that be not as though they were according to Romans 4:17c.

As soon as I got home I started reading and began digging out the healing scriptures and compiling them into my very own document which I entitled "My Daily Bread". After compiling them, I began to speak them over myself daily for months and have continued this practice for the intervening years.

I am including this document here because it was the very first of many that I compiled and began confessing each morning in my devotional time. I had learned that the words I was speaking were going to bring about life and health so the fifteen minutes it took to speak it out every day was a worthy investment of my time~ and in time it brought forth what the word said I already had, healing, wholeness, blessing and life! May it be unto you as well!

My Daily Bread
To you O LORD I lift up my soul. Psalm 25:1

Our Father who art in heaven, hallowed be thy name. Thy Kingdom come, thy will be done, on earth as *it is* in heaven. Give us this day our daily bread and forgive us our trespasses as we forgive those who trespass against us. Lead us not into temptation but deliver us from evil, for thine is the kingdom and the power and the glory forever. Amen. Matthew 6:9-13

Praise the LORD O my soul, all my inmost being, praise his holy name. Praise the LORD O my soul and forget not all his benefits- who forgives all your sins and heals all your diseases.
Psalm 103:1-3

Surely he took up our infirmities and carried our sorrows, yet we considered him stricken by God, smitten by him and afflicted. But he was pierced for our iniquities, the punishment that brought us peace was upon him and by his wounds we are healed.
Isaiah 53:4-5

He took up our infirmities and carried our diseases.
Matthew 8:17b

He himself bore our sins in his body on the tree, so that we might die to sins and live for righteousness, it's by his wounds that you have been healed. 1 Peter 2:24

He heals the brokenhearted and binds up their wounds.
Psalm 147:3

He sent forth his word and healed them, he rescued them from the grave. Psalm 107:20

I have heard your prayer and seen your tears, I will heal you.
2 Kings 20:5b

O LORD my GOD, I called to you for help and you healed me. Psalm 30:2

I will restore you to health and heal your wounds, declares the LORD. Jeremiah 30:17a

Worship the LORD your God and his blessing will be on your food and water. I will take away sickness from among you. Exodus 23:25

And the prayer offered in faith will make the sick person well, the Lord will raise him up. James 5:15a

I will not die but live, and will proclaim what the LORD has done. Psalm 118:17

But for you who revere my name, the sun of righteousness will rise with healing in its wings. And you will go out and leap like calves released from the stall. Malachi 4:2

Do not be wise in your own eyes, fear the LORD and shun evil. This will bring health to your body and nourishment to your bones. Proverbs 3:7-8

My son, pay attention to what I say, listen closely to my words. Do not let them out of your sight, keep them within your heart for they are life to those who find them and to a mans whole body. Proverbs 4:20-22

The LORD will keep you free from every disease. Deuteronomy 7:15a

So tell them, 'as surely as I live, declares the LORD, I will do to you the very things I heard you say. Numbers 14:28 (this one blew my mind)

... I tell you the truth, if you have faith as small as a mustard seed, you can say to this mountain, 'move from here to there' and it will move. Nothing will be impossible for you." Matthew 17:20b

No weapon formed against you will prevail, and you will refute every tongue that accuses you. This is the heritage of the servants of the LORD, and this is their vindication from me" declares the LORD. Isaiah 54:17

So is my word that goes out from my mouth: It will not return to me empty, but will accomplish what I desire and achieve the purpose for which I sent it. Isaiah 55:11

The God who gives life to the dead and calls things that are not as though they were. Romans 4:17b

For we are God's workmanship, created in Christ Jesus to do good works, which God prepared in advance for us to do. Ephesians 2:10

And my God will meet all your needs according to his glorious riches in Christ Jesus. Philippians 4:19

For he has rescued us from the dominion of darkness and brought us into the kingdom of the Son he loves, in whom we have redemption, the forgiveness of sins. Colossians 1:13-14

You, dear children, are from God and have overcome them, because the one who is in you is greater than the one who is in the world. 1 John 4:4

Dear friend, I pray that you may enjoy good health and that all may go well with you, even as your soul is getting along well. 3 John 2

The Lord is my Shepherd, I shall not be in want. Psalm 23:1

The LORD will grant that the enemies who rise up against you will be defeated before you. They will come at you from one direction but flee from you in seven. Deuteronomy 28:7

Go into all the world and preach the good news to all creation. Whoever believes and is baptized will be saved, but whoever does not believe will be condemned. And these signs will accompany those who believe: In my name they will drive out demons, they will speak in new tongues, they will pick up snakes with their hands and when they drink deadly poison, it will not hurt them at all, they will place their hands on sick people and they will get well. Mark 16:15-18

I have given you authority to trample on snakes and scorpions and to overcome all the power of the enemy, nothing by any means will harm you. Luke 10:19

The Spirit of the Lord is on me, because he has anointed me to preach the good news to the poor. He has sent me to proclaim freedom for the prisoners and recovery of sight to the blind, to release the oppressed, to proclaim the year of the Lord's favor. Luke 4:18-19

As you go, preach this message: "The kingdom of heaven is near." Heal the sick, raise the dead, cleanse those who have leprosy, drive out demons. Freely you have received, freely give. Matthew 10:7

The Lord will rescue me from every evil attack and will bring me safely to his heavenly kingdom. To him be the glory forever and ever. Amen! 2 Timothy 4:18

They overcame him by the blood of the Lamb and by the word of their testimony. Revelation 12:11a

But seek first his kingdom and his righteousness, and all these things will be given to you as well. Matthew 6:33

The weapons we fight with are not the weapons of the world. On the contrary, they have divine power to demolish strongholds. We demolish arguments and every pretension that sets itself up against the knowledge of God and we take captive every thought to make it obedient to Christ. 2 Corinthians 10:4-5

The thief comes only to steal kill and destroy, I have come that they may have life, and have it to the full. John 10:10

For everyone who asks receives, he who seeks finds and to him who knocks, the door will be opened. Luke 11:10

I tell you the truth, anyone who has faith in me will do what I have been doing. He will do even greater things than these, because I am going to the Father. John 14:12

If you remain in me and my words remain in you, ask whatever you wish, and it will be given you. John 15:7

The Spirit gives life, the flesh counts for nothing. The words I have spoken to you are spirit and they are life. John 6:63

A cheerful heart is good medicine, but a crushed spirit dries up the bones. Proverbs 17:22

The fear of the LORD adds length to life, but the years of the wicked are cut short. Proverbs 10:27

Reckless words pierce like a sword, but the tongue of the wise brings healing. Proverbs 12:18

The tongue that brings healing is a tree of life, but a deceitful tongue crushes the spirit. Proverbs 15:4

Commit to the LORD whatever you do, and your plans will succeed. Proverbs 16:3

Praise be to the Lord, to God our Savior, who daily bears our burdens. Psalm 68:19

Blessed are all who fear the LORD, who walk in his ways. You will eat the fruit of your labor, blessings and prosperity will be yours. Psalm 128:1-2

The LORD is my rock, my fortress and my deliverer; my God is my rock, in whom I take refuge. I call to the LORD, who is worthy of praise and I am saved from my enemies. Psalm 18:2a-3

Cast your cares on the LORD and he will sustain you.
Psalm 55:22a

I can do all *things* through Christ who strengthens me.
Philippians 4:13

So do not fear for I am with you, do not be dismayed, for I am your God. I will strengthen you and help you, I will uphold you with my righteous right hand. Isaiah 41:10

The tongue has the power of life and death, and those who love it will eat its fruit. Proverbs 18:21

For the LORD God is a sun and a shield, the LORD bestows favor and honor, no good thing does he withhold from those whose walk is blameless. Psalm 84:11

Now may the Lord's strength be displayed, just as you have declared. Numbers 14:17

Jesus answered, "It is written: 'man does not live on bread alone, but on every word that proceeds from the mouth of God.'" Matthew 4:4

To the man who pleases him, God gives wisdom, knowledge and happiness… Ecclesiastes 2:26a

For I know the plans I have for you declares the LORD, plans to prosper you and not to harm you, plans to give you a hope and a future." Then you will call upon me and come and pray to me and I will listen to you. You will seek me and find me when you seek me with all your heart. Jeremiah 29:11-13

Let us then approach the throne of grace with confidence, so that we may receive mercy and find grace to help us in our time of need. Hebrews 4:16

Cast your bread upon the waters, for after many days you will find it again. Ecclesiastes 11:1

The prince of this world now stands condemned. John 16:11b

Take heart! I have overcome the world. John 16:33

Come near to God and he will come near to you. James 4:8a

Jesus Christ is the same yesterday and today and forever. Hebrews 13:8

Praise be to the God and Father of our Lord Jesus Christ, who has blessed us in the heavenly realms with every spiritual blessing in Christ. Ephesians 1:3

Therefore God exalted to the highest place and gave him the name that is above every name, that at the name of Jesus, every knee should bow, in heaven and on earth and under the earth. Philippians 2:9-10

The LORD is my Shepherd, I shall not be in want. He maketh me to lie down in green pastures, he leadeth me beside the still waters. He restoreth my soul, he leadeth me in the paths of righteousness for his name's sake. Yea, though I walk through the valley of the shadow of death, I will fear no evil for thou art with me, thy rod and thy staff, they comfort me. Thou preparest a table before me in the presence of mine enemies, thou anointest my head with oil, my cup runneth over. Surely goodness and mercy shall follow me all the days of my life, and I will dwell in the house of the LORD for ever. Psalm 23:1-6 (KJV)

It is of the LORD'S mercies that we are not consumed because his compassions fail not. *They are* new every morning, great *is* thy faithfulness. The LORD *is* my portion saith my soul, therefore will I hope in him. Lamentations 3:22-24 (KJV)

Let nothing move you. Always give yourselves fully to the work of the Lord because you know that your labor is not in vain. 1 Corinthians 15:58b

Your word, O LORD, is eternal, it stands firm in the heavens. Psalm 119:89

Never will I leave you, never will I forsake you. Hebrews 13:5b

Trust in the LORD with all your heart and lean not on your own understanding, in all your ways acknowledge him and he will make your paths straight. Proverbs 3:5

It's not by might nor by power, but by my Spirit says the Lord Almighty. Zechariah 4:6b

I pray also that the eyes of your heart may be enlightened in order that you may know the hope to which he has called you, the riches of his glorious inheritance in the saints, and his incomparably great power for us who believe. That power is like the working of his mighty strength, which he exerted in Christ when he raised him from the dead and seated him at his right hand in the heavenly realms. Ephesians 1:18-20

L.A.Mars 2005

Faith Talk

"Faith Talk" was my favorite topic we taught. It was through teaching it to others that God's word became real and alive in me. You may remember that old song, Standing on the Promises of God, Russell K. Carter penned this hymn in 1886 based upon the words in Hebrews 10:23 ~ Let us hold unswervingly to the hope we profess, for he who promised is faithful.

Little did I know then that I was about to embark on a journey "to *know him more*" and his faithfulness. For about the next year I really practiced this "standing on the word". I put together several documents including one entitled "Jesus you are", specifically denoting who and what Jesus was and is to me. As I called out to him daily I would bring to his remembrance his promises to me and it was through this simple daily exercise that I truly began to place my faith and trust in the Lord. I also put together pages of scriptures concerning my marriage and various other topics which I have included in the index for your use.

In early 2006 I recorded several of these confessions so I could have it playing in my home, all day, every day, 24/7, just as I had done with Jake in the hospital. I was beginning to understand and see just how important speaking the word of God really was. In addition to that, I was also seeing how powerful his word was to bring about changes in my life. I can say with confidence that I was truly beginning to "*know him more*". I gave Linda a copy of this recording to take along on a mission trip to a place where the gospel is not allowed, she too was encouraged to hear the word of God in a familiar voice which brought her great comfort in a very difficult situation. Hallelujah!

I became so hungry for the word of God and seeing his power manifest that I began attending Healing Services all around the cities. I got involved with the Healing Rooms of St. Paul and started attending a weekly Healing School held at Living Word Church. I attended the International Healing Conferences, DSMI (Doug Stanton) and HEMI, (Harold Eatmon) where I met others who were also involved with healing and deliverance ministries.

We also participated in a couple of the Worldwide Day's of Healing that Charles and Francis Hunter coordinated which opened the door for Greater Works Ministries to also begin holding monthly healing services. Can you guess where we held the meetings? Yep, it was at the local Curves where Linda and Liz first met and prayed together!

God used all of this to raise up the Greater Works Ministries Healing School. I was not only beginning to see that my Heavenly Father was a wonderful planner, administrator and provider, I now knew without a doubt that he was and is, Hallelujah!

I not only read every book on healing that I could get my hands on during this time, I also completed a three year correspondence course through Ken Hagen's RHEMA Bible School. A little more recently in 2012 I was Certified as a Prayer Minister through Christians' United Ministries and began working with prayer clients on a weekly basis.

I have continued to see God's people delivered, protected, healed, preserved, blessed to do well and be made whole in Jesus name, all to the glory of God! Hallelujah! In February of 2014 I became a licensed and ordained minister through Christians United Ministries.

In the past ten years I have seen many people instantly healed in their bodies and made whole through the laying on of hands. I have seen others struggle to obtain their healing, I have seen some walk away in doubt and unbelief and I have seen some persevere till the end and go home to heaven instead. I yet have a desire to see the lame walk, the deaf hear and the dead be raised, I trust you do too!

Although I had learned so much by this time, I discovered that I also needed to learn who I was in Christ so that the enemies lies would no longer prevail in my life, I needed to continue hiding God's word in my heart so that I would not sin against him as Psalm 119:11 encourages us. By his grace I continue to do so, Amen.

Yet another great teaching from the Healing School that encouraged me greatly was entitled "Confession". When most of us hear the word "confession" we think of confessing our sins or those feelings of guilt that come because we have done something wrong. Although this may be true, there is another meaning to be understood that I'd like to share with you and if you'll permit it to, it will (trust me) bring about transformation in your life as it did mine and countless others. Below I have included the Strong's Concordance references from both the New Testament in Greek and the Old Testament in Hebrew.

Strong's G.3670 - homologeo ~ to confess, acknowledge, agree, admit, declare~ this can be a profession of allegiance, an admission of bad behavior, or *an emphatic declaration of a truth-*

Strong's H.3034 - yada ~ to shoot (a bow) to throw (down); to express praise, give thanks, extol, make a public confession, make an admission; to praise is to speak of the excellence of someone or something, to give thanks has a focus on the gratitude of the speaker.

As you will see declaring the emphatic truth of God's word is what positive confession looks like. When we agree with God's word we can emphatically declare it for ourselves! Be warned, the enemy will be close by whispering that it's not true. Be encouraged though, if we find it in God's word we know that it's the truth, so let's declare it! The Bible has a lot more to say about it so please refer to the index for the complete teaching on *"Confession"*.

Upon learning about this confession stuff, I was very excited to create a document entitled *"I Am"* which describes who I am as a child of God and exactly what my inheritance in Christ included, it's what this book is all about. You may be familiar with some of the more common scriptures describing who we are in Christ like Isaiah 43:4 ~ I am precious in his sight or Philippians 4:13 ~ I am able to do all things through Christ who strengthens me, or others like, I am chosen, I am beloved, I am an ambassador of Christ and so on.

As I continued in God's word I was set free by knowing the truth of who I was in him! As I was set free by confessing and knowing in my knower (my heart) these truths, I would encourage others with these same truths and watch the truth set them free too!

Jesus said in John 8:31b-32~ If you continue in my word, then you are truly disciples of mine, and you will know the truth and the truth will make you free. Our part is clear, we must continue in his word and as we do, we will know the truth, (that's Jesus) and then that truth, (that's Jesus) will set us free, Amen and Amen!

What follows is the very first *"I Am"* document I put together for myself and subsequently used for the Healing School. Once again, as I would confess these truths daily and according to Psalm 119:11, I was beginning to hide God's word in my heart so that I would not sin against him, I now invite you to do the same!

"To know him more" ~ The LORD and his word are truly powerful to transform lives just like ours and according to scripture, he will also watch over his word to perform it. When we do our part, by hiding his word in our hearts, then he will do his part (the transformation) and give us the new life we long for and that he so dearly paid for!

* I AM *

I am redeemed forgiven of my sin - Ephesians 1:7
I am forgiven, cleansed from all unrighteousness - 1 John 1:9
I am a new creation, the old is gone the new
  is come - 2 Corinthians 5:17
I am a temple of the Holy Spirit - 1 Corinthians 6:19
I am redeemed from the curse of the law - Galatians 3:13
I am part of a chosen race, a royal priesthood, a holy nation,
  God's own people - 1 Peter 2:9
I am chosen from before the foundation of the world - Ephesians 1:4
I am his disciple and his truth sets me free - John 8:31-32
I am strong in the Lord and in the strength of
  his might - Ephesians 6:10
I am united with him in his death, so I can be united with
  him in his resurrection - Romans 6:5
I am more than a conqueror through Christ - Romans 8:37
I am a child of God and a fellow heir with Christ - Romans 8:16-17
I am sealed with his Holy Spirit, the guarantee of his
  inheritance - Ephesians 1:13-14
I am crucified with Christ and I no longer live, but Christ
  lives in me - Galatians 2:20
I am loved by God and made alive with Christ - Ephesians 2:4-5
I am alive in him and forgiven of all my sin - Colossians 2:13
I am promised eternal life - John 6:47
I am reconciled to God through Christ - 2 Corinthians 5:18
I am qualified to share in the inheritance of
  the saints - Colossians 1:12

I am no longer a stranger, but a fellow citizen and a member
of God's household - Ephesians 2:19
I am his treasured possession - Deuteronomy 14:2
I am blessed with every spiritual blessing in Christ - Ephesians 1:3
I am loved so individually that he's even counted the hairs
on my head - Matthew 10:30
I am the righteousness of God because Jesus became
sin for me - 2 Corinthians 5:21
I am saved and called, not by my works, but because of his
own purpose and grace - 2 Timothy 1:9
I am beloved by God and chosen by him - 1 Thessalonians 1:4
I am an ambassador for Christ - 2 Corinthians 5:20
I am his workmanship created in Christ Jesus - Ephesians 2:10
I am the apple of his eye - Zechariah 2:8
I am being changed into his likeness with ever
increasing glory - 2 Corinthians 3:18
I am reconciled to him so I can be holy, blameless and
irreproachable before him - Colossians 1:22
I am promised that he will complete the work he has begun
in me - Philippians 1:6
I am a possessor of eternal life - John 5:24
I am able to draw near to his throne of grace to receive mercy
and grace in time of need - Hebrews 4:16
I am a citizen of heaven and Jesus is my Savior - Philippians 3:20
I am raised up with him and sit with him in the heavenly
places - Ephesians 2:6
I am a gift to Jesus from God himself and he will
not cast me out - John 6:37
I am with Jesus whether I am awake or asleep - 1 Thessalonians 5:10
I am of God and he who is in me is greater than he who is
in the world - 1 John 4:4
I am a child of God and he loves me - 1 John 3:1
I am not my own, I was bought with a price - 1 Corinthians 6:19
I am no longer a slave but a son and an heir - Galatians 4:7
I am no longer dead in my sins but alive with Christ - Colossians 2:13
I am Christ's friend - John 15:15
I am Justified - Romans 5:1

I am united with the Lord and one with him
  in Spirit - 1 Corinthians 6:17
I am a member of Christ's body - 1 Corinthians 12:27
I am a saint - Ephesians 1:1
I am adopted as God's child - Ephesians 1:5
I am complete in Christ - Colossians 2:10
I am free forever from condemnation - Romans 8:1
I am established, anointed and sealed by God - 2 Corinthians 1:21
I am hidden with Christ in God - Colossians 3:3
I am free from any condemning charges against me - Romans 8:33
I am assured that all things work together for good - Romans 8:28
I am the salt and light of the earth - Matthew 5:13
I am a branch of the true vine - John 15:1
I am chosen and appointed to bear fruit - John 15:16
I am a personal witness of Christ's - Acts 1:8
I am a minister of reconciliation - 2 Corinthians 5:18
I am God's co-worker - 2 Corinthians 6:1
I am able to do all things through Christ who strengthens
  me - Philippians 4:13
I am born again, not of perishable seed, but of
  imperishable seed - 1 Peter 1:23
I am convinced that nothing will be able to separate me from
  the love of God - Romans 8:38
I am an inheritor of eternal life, I will never perish and no one
  can snatch me out of his hand - John 10:28
I am delivered from the dominion of darkness - Colossians 1:13
I am transferred to the kingdom of his beloved Son - Colossians 1:13
I am ransomed from the futile ways inherited from my fathers
  by his holy and precious blood - 1 Peter 1:18-19
I am the head and not the tail - Deuteronomy 28:13a
I am an over-comer by the blood of the Lamb - Revelation 12:11
I am free - Romans 6:18
I am given weapons to demolish strongholds - 2 Corinthians 10:4
I am being inwardly renewed day by day - 2 Corinthians 4:16
I am fixing my eyes on what is unseen - 2 Corinthians 4:18
I am endued with power from on high - Luke 24:49 & Acts 2:4
I am free from every disease - Deuteronomy 7:15a

I am not consumed because his compassions fail
  not - Lamentations 3:22
I am anointed to preach the good news to the poor - Luke 4:18
I am rescued from every evil attack - 2 Timothy 4:18
I am clean because of the word Jesus has spoken to me - John 15:3
I am preaching, healing, raising the dead and driving out
  demons - Matthew 10:7
I am placing my hands on sick people and they do get
  well - Mark 16:18
I am supplied with all I need according to his riches in glory in
  Christ Jesus - Philippians 4:19
I am given everything I need for life and godliness through my
  knowledge of Jesus - 2 Peter 1:3
I am not in want - Psalm 23:1

*Please refer to the Bible reference for complete scriptures

L.A. Mars 2005

As a disciple of Jesus the Christ, it is vitally important to know who we are in him. As time went on and I learned more about who I was in Christ, I would add those scriptures to my on-going list. One day, somebody asked if I was going to write a book with all those "*I Am's*", I kind of laughed and thought that that would be cool, but... I really had no plans of doing so. As the years rolled on I continued to come across scriptures that were relevant so I would add them. At some point it was becoming difficult to add new verses because I had to search all the pages to see if I had already added them. It was then that I decided to organize them by putting them into chronological order. That task took some time to accomplish, however, the time I spent doing it has proven very valuable. I was now able to quickly see if verses were there or not. Little did I know that one day~ the Lord, my Papa, would encourage me to "write that book".

In 2009 I decided to read through the book of Romans with the intent of searching for verses that I could personalize and add, then two years later during a women's bible study on the book of Ephesians it became apparent to me that I would create a comprehensive list for this book as well. There were numerous verses to personalize, many of which were documented already. As I would read, I kept paper and pencil next to me and as the Holy Spirit enlightened me I would personalize the verses by writing it out (long hand) and when I had accumulated a full page, I'd type them up. I'm not sure about you, but something happens inside of me when I take the time to *write* out the scripture verses, you should try it some time! According to Psalm 119:11, there I was again, hiding God's word in my heart so that I would not sin against him. Due to my earlier cataloging it was no problem to insert the Ephesians verses where they needed to be. It was at this time in 2011 that I had some thoughts that maybe, just maybe~ maybe someday, I would turn it all into a book.

Let's fast forward to November of 2012. It was at this time that Father God spoke to me concerning the writing of this book. I was at a Saturday morning meeting over at North Heights and what follows is in part some of the dialog we had. As I was journaling that day I was amazed as Father God spoke this to me~

"Be holy as I am holy ~ I am the GREAT I AM ~ write that book ~ focus on me ~ fill your empty places with me for I am yours in abundance ~ in love I created you for such a time as this ~"

It was then with the Fathers prompting that I methodically began reading the New Testament and then the Old Testament searching for verses containing the promises of who *"I Am"* in him to personalize. Along the way the Holy Spirit also began enlightening me with the verses that were describing God the Father, God the Son and God the Holy Spirit, all three *"I AM's"*! You will note that I use all capital letters when the verses are referring to God and lower case ones to describe who and or what we have in him.

Some have struggled with the concept of personalizing the scriptures stating that this would violate Gods word found in Revelation 22:18-19 that admonishes us to not change the scriptures. If we read these verses correctly we will see that the scripture is not talking about changing words, rather, it's talking about adding to or taking away from the prophecies found therein.

I testify to everyone who hears the words of the prophecy of this book: if anyone adds to them, God will add to him the plagues which are written in this book, and if anyone takes away from the words of the book of this prophecy, God will take away his part from the tree of life and from the holy city which are written in

this book. Revelation 22:18-19

In no way by personalizing the scriptures am I adding to or deleting from or changing any doctrine or prophecy there-in. If you are an individual who struggles with this concept I pray you will move forward in seeing the truth presented here, search out the scriptures for yourself while being open to see that what I am doing is personalizing and claiming the scriptures for myself as led by the Holy Spirit. As a blood bought child of the Most High God I desire to know who "*I am*" and what my inheritance in Christ includes. I pray that you, the reader, will begin to declare the emphatic truths of God's word while confessing it for and over yourself so that you too may bear witness to God's powerful transformative power in your own life and in the lives of others! Be careful though, this is not a name it and claim it formula~ rather may it be as according to Romans 4:17c, **calling those things that be not as though they are.**

When I created this first "*I Am*" document I was using the New International Version. It was in 2007 that I began using the New American Standard Version. Therefore, I would encourage you to look up the verses in your own version which may or may not differ from what I have used. Although I have read through the entire bible (multiple times for this book) it is very likely that this is not an exhaustive list. As you read and search the scriptures for yourself, I pray that with the Holy Spirits enlightenment you will add your own verses as he reveals them to you, why? Because you are his precious one!

I also encourage that as you begin to read the following pages that you will take a marking pen of some kind and begin to highlight the verses that the Holy Spirit quickens to you. I further pray that you will begin to create your own *"I Am's"* and or confession lists and begin declaring the emphatic truth of Gods word over your life and situations. (I know, I know, I know, I just said that. In the scriptures when something is repeated, we are to realize the strong admonition to pay very careful attention to it. *lol*)

Just yesterday I met with Linda, my sister and friend in the Lord, she told me that just a couple of weeks ago she gave someone a copy of that original *"I Am"* document. Although written years ago, what a testimony of Hebrews 4:12a ~ **For the word of God is living and active and sharper than any double edged sword.**

I pray you will be blessed as you search these promises of scripture. As you fulfill God's will for your life according to Romans 8:28-30 **That the God of all glory will transform you into the image of his Son, our Savior ~ Jesus.**

3 John 1:2 ~ **Beloved, I pray that in all respects that you may prosper and be in good health, just as your soul prospers.**

WARNING

(Proceeding from here will change your life)

In the following pages you'll find the entirety of the *"I Am's"* including the *"I AM's"* that declare who and or what God is and does.

I trust as you lean in God will teach you as he has me~ just who and whose you are as well as what your great and glorious inheritance is because of his great love for you, for he truly is the *"GREAT I AM"*!

I cannot emphasize it enough~ please do not skip over these pages. Let me encourage you to take the time to not only read these verses, I am also encouraging you to read them out loud as well, especially if you want to stand your ground and kick the devil around a bit!

This is not a name it and claim it gimmick, God's word really works! When I was in A.A. decades ago there was a saying that I think is appropriate here. At the conclusion of our meetings we would say, *"It works if you work it!"* So whether you read it aloud or silently, you will be hiding God's word in your heart so that you will not sin against him, moreover, you will begin to appropriate Gods blessings for your life as well and come to know what your inheritance is, not to mention that you will be on your way to *"knowing him more"*.

As you continue, I call you to remember this, that Jesus not only came to give us life, he came to give it to us in abundance! So~ go get it!

It Works ~ if You Work It!

I pray for a spirit of wisdom and revelation so that I may know you better and that the eyes of
my heart might be enlightened to know the hope to which I am called. Ephesians 1:17-19
I pray that out of your glorious riches you may strengthen me with power through your
Spirit in my inner being so that Christ may dwell in my heart. Ephesians 3:16-17

* I AM *

I am patient, I am kind, I do not envy, I do not boast, I am not proud, I am not rude,
I am not self seeking, I am not easily angered. I keep no record of wrongs, I do not delight in evil,
I rejoice in the truth. I always protect, always trust, always hope, always persevere.
{I bear, believe, hope and endure all things}
1 Corinthians 13:4-7

I am created in his image and likeness - Genesis 1:26

I am earnestly heeding the voice of the Lord my God - Exodus 15:26a
I am doing what is right in his sight - Exodus 15:26b
I am giving ear to his commands and I am keeping
his statutes - Exodus 15:26c
I AM is the Lord my healer - Exodus 15:26e
I AM rains down the bread from heaven - Exodus 16:4
I AM gives us meat to eat in the evening and bread to eat
in the morning - Exodus 16:8b

I am holy because the Lord my God is holy - Leviticus 19:2
I am respecting my mother and father - Leviticus 19:3a
I am observing the Sabbath - Leviticus 19:3b
I AM is the Lord my God - Leviticus 19:3c
I am not turning to idols or making molten gods - Leviticus 19:4
I am not stealing, lying or being deceptive - Leviticus 19:11
I am not profaning the name of the Lord - Leviticus 19:12
I am not defrauding my neighbor or robbing him or holding
back wages - Leviticus 19:13
I am not cursing the deaf nor putting stumbling blocks in front
of the blind - Leviticus 19:14a
I am fearing my God, I AM is the Lord - Leviticus 19:14b
I am not perverting justice or showing partiality or favoritism
and I judge my neighbor fairly - Leviticus 19:15
I am not going about spreading slander or endangering
my neighbor's life - Leviticus 19:16

I am not hating my brother, I rebuke my neighbor frankly
   so I do not share his guilt - Leviticus 19:17
I am not seeking revenge or bearing grudges - Leviticus 19:18a
I am loving my neighbor as myself - Leviticus 19:18b
I am keeping God's decrees and not mating different
   kinds of animals - Leviticus 19:19a
I am not planting my field with two kinds of seeds - Leviticus 19:19b
I am not wearing clothing woven of two kinds of
   material - Leviticus 19:19c
I am not eating any meat with the blood still in it - Leviticus 19:26a
I am not practicing divination or sorcery - Leviticus 19:26b
I am not cutting the hair at the sides of my head or clipping
   the edges of my beard - Leviticus 19:27
I am not cutting my body or putting tattoos on it - Leviticus 19:28
I am not degrading my daughter by making her a
   prostitute - Leviticus 19:29
I am observing the Sabbath and have reverence for
   Gods' sanctuary - Leviticus 19:30
I am not turning to mediums or spiritists - Leviticus 19:31
I am rising in the presence of the elderly and revering
   God - Leviticus 19:32
I am not mistreating aliens - Leviticus 19:33
I am loving the aliens as I love myself - Leviticus 19:34
I am not using dishonest standards when measuring length,
   weight or quantity - Leviticus 19:35
I am using honest scales and honest weights - Leviticus 19:36
I am keeping and following all of Gods decrees
   and laws - Leviticus 19:37
I AM broke the yoke bars and has enabled me to walk with
   my head held high - Leviticus 26:13b

I AM is slow to anger and abounding in love - Numbers 14:18a
I AM forgives sin, transgression and iniquity yet he does not
   leave the guilty unpunished - Numbers 14:18b
I AM will do to me the very things he hears me say - Numbers 14:28
I AM is not a man that he should lie, nor a son of man that
   he should change his mind - Numbers 23:19

I am not having any other gods before me - Deuteronomy 5:7
I am not making for myself any idols - Deuteronomy 5:8
I am not taking the name of the Lord my God
  in vain - Deuteronomy 5:11
I am observing the Sabbath day, keeping it holy - Deuteronomy 5:12
I am honoring my father and mother - Deuteronomy 5:16
I am not murdering - Deuteronomy 5:17
I am not committing adultery - Deuteronomy 5:18
I am not stealing - Deuteronomy 5:19
I am not bearing false witness against my
  neighbor - Deuteronomy 5:20
I am not coveting my neighbor's house, wife, servant, animals
  or anything that belongs to them - Deuteronomy 5:21
I am loving the Lord my God with all my heart, soul
  and might - Deuteronomy 6:5
I am teaching these words to my sons and talking of them
  when I sit, when I walk by the way and when I lie down
  and when I rise up - Deuteronomy 6:7
I am binding them as a sign on my hands and my
  forehead - Deuteronomy 6:8
I am writing them on the doorposts of my house and on
  my gates - Deuteronomy 6:9
I am fearing the Lord my God, I worship him and swear
  by his name - Deuteronomy 6:13
I am not following any other gods - Deuteronomy 6:14
I AM is in our midst and he is a jealous God - Deuteronomy 6:15
I am free from every disease - Deuteronomy 7:15a
I AM is a great and awesome God - Deuteronomy 7:21
I AM disciplines me as a man disciplines his son - Deuteronomy 8:5
I am keeping the commandments of the Lord my
  God - Deuteronomy 8:6a
I am walking in his ways and fearing him - Deuteronomy 8:6b
I AM the Lord my God is a consuming fire - Deuteronomy 9:3
I am fearing the Lord, walking in his ways, loving and serving
  him with all my heart and soul - Deuteronomy 10:12
I AM is the God of gods and Lord of lords, the great, the mighty
  and the awesome God who does not show partiality nor take

a bribe - Deuteronomy 10:17

I AM executes justice for orphan's and widows, he shows love to the alien by giving him food and clothing - Deuteronomy 10:18

I am following the Lord my god, fearing him and I am keeping his commandments - Deuteronomy 13:4a

I am listening to his voice, I am serving and clinging to him - Deuteronomy 13:4b

I am his chosen possession - Deuteronomy 14:2

I AM is our inheritance - Deuteronomy 18:2

I am declaring this day that the Lord is my God and that I will walk in his way, keeping his decrees, commands and laws - Deuteronomy 26:17

I am his treasured possession - Deuteronomy 26:18

I am diligently obeying the Lord and being careful to do all his commandments then the Lord will set me high above all the nations on earth - Deuteronomy 28:1

I am blessed in the city and I am blesses me in the country - Deuteronomy 28:3

I AM blesses the offspring of my body, my produce, my beasts, the increase of herd and their flock - Deuteronomy 28:4

I AM blesses my basket and kneading trough - Deuteronomy 28:5

I am blessed when I come in and when I go out - Deuteronomy 28:6

I AM blesses my barn and everything I put my hand to - Deuteronomy 28:8

I AM will establish me if I keep his commands and walk in his ways - Deuteronomy 28:9

I AM opens for me the heavens to give rain and to bless the work of my hands - Deuteronomy 28:12a

I am a lender and not a borrower - Deuteronomy 28:12b

I am the head and not the tail - Deuteronomy 28:13a

I am not turning aside from his commands - Deuteronomy 28:14

I AM rejoices over me for good - Deuteronomy 30:9c

I am choosing life and blessings today so that I and my descendants may live long - Deuteronomy 30:19b

I am loving the Lord and obeying his voice and holding fast to him - Deuteronomy 30:20

I am strong and courageous, not afraid because the LORD

my God is the one who goes with me - Deuteronomy 31:6a
I AM will not fail or forsake me - Deuteronomy 31:6b
I AM is the Rock! His work is perfect - Deuteronomy 32:4a
I AM is just, faithful and righteous - Deuteronomy 32:4b
I am the Lord's portion - Deuteronomy 32:9a
I AM encircles, cares for and guards me as the pupil
  of his eye - Deuteronomy 32:10

I am given everywhere I set my feet - Joshua 1:3
I am never left or forsaken - Joshua 1:5
I am never left or forsaken - Joshua 1:6

I am strong and very courageous, careful to obey the law,
  not turning to the right or the left that I may be successful
  wherever I go - Joshua 1:7
I am meditating on the law day and night not letting it
  depart from my mouth - Joshua 1:8a
I am careful to do everything written in the book of the
  law that I may be prosperous and successful - Joshua 1:8b
I am, me and my household are serving the LORD - Joshua 24:15

I am the apple of his eye - Zechariah 2:8

I AM delivers the afflicted in their affliction and opens our
  ears in times of oppression - Job 36:15
I AM does great things which we cannot comprehend - Job 37:5b
I AM is perfect in knowledge - Job 37:16
I AM comes in awesome majesty - Job 37:22b

I AM can do all things and no purpose of his can
  be thwarted - Job 42:2
I am blessed because I do not walk in the council of the
  wicked or stand in the path of sinners or sit in the seat
  of mockers - Psalm 1:1
I am delighting in the law of the Lord - Psalm 1:2a
I am meditating on his law day and night - Psalm 1:2b
I am like a tree planted by the water - Psalm 1:3a

I am prospering in whatever I do - Psalm 1:3c
I am serving the Lord with reverence and I rejoice
  with trembling - Psalm 2:11a
I am blessed because I take refuge in him - Psalm 2:12c
I am sustained by the Lord - Psalm 3:5b
I am not afraid of ten thousands of people set against me - Psalm 3:6
I am relieved in my stress - Psalm 4:1b
I am set apart for the Lord - Psalm 4:3a
I am heard when I call out to him - Psalm 4:3b
I am still as I meditate in my heart upon my bed - Psalm 4:4
I am offering sacrifices of righteousness and trust in
  the Lord - Psalm 4:5
I am lying down and sleeping in peace - Psalm 4:8a
I am dwelling in safety - Psalm 4:8b
I am ordering my prayer to you in the morning and
  eagerly watch - Psalm 5:3
I am surrounded by God's favor as with a shield - Psalm 5:12b
I am made a little lower than the heavenly beings and
  crowned with glory and honor - Psalm 8:5
I am praising you O Lord with all my heart and telling
  of all your wonders - Psalm 9:1
I am glad and rejoice in you, I will sing to your name,
  O Most High - Psalm 9:2
I AM the LORD is King forever and ever - Psalm 10:16a
I AM hears the desires of the afflicted and encourages
  them - Psalm 10:17
I AM defends the fatherless and the oppressed - Psalm 10:18
I AM observes and examines the sons of men - Psalm 11:4b
I AM the LORD is righteous, he loves justice and upright
  men will see his face - Psalm 11:7
I am trusting in your unfailing love, my heart rejoices
  in your salvation - Psalm 13:5
I am singing to the Lord for he has been good to me - Psalm 13:6
I am is my LORD and apart from him I have no good
  thing - Psalm 16:2
I AM assigns me my portion and cup, he has made
  my lot secure - Psalm 16:5

I AM councils me, even at night my heart instructs me - Psalm 16:7
I am always setting the LORD before me, because he is
  my right hand I will not be shaken - Psalm 16:8
I am rejoicing and my heart is glad, my body rests secure - Psalm 16:9
I AM makes known to me the path of life, fills me with
  joy in his presence with eternal pleasures - Psalm 16:11
I AM probes my heart and examines me at night - Psalm 17:3a
I am resolving that my mouth will not sin - Psalm 17:3c
I am keeping myself from the ways of the violent,
  my steps hold to your path - Psalm 17:4b
I am holding my steps to your path - Psalm 17:5
I am calling upon you O Lord for you will answer me - Psalm 17:6
I AM shows us his loving-kindness - Psalm 17:7a
I am taking refuge at his right hand - Psalm 17:7b
I am kept as the apple of his eye - Psalm 17:8a
I am hidden in the shadow of your wings - Psalm 17:8b
I AM is my rock, my fortress and my deliverer in whom I take
  refuge, he is my shield and the horn of my salvation - Psalm 18:2
I am calling to the LORD who is worthy to be praised and I
  am saved from my enemies - Psalm 18:3
I AM reaches down from on high and takes hold of me,
  drawing me out of deep waters - Psalm 18:16
I AM rescues me from my powerful enemy, the foes who
  are to strong for me - Psalm 18:17
I AM the LORD is my support - Psalm 18:18

I AM brings me out into a spacious place, he rescued me
  because he delights in me - Psalm 18:19
I AM deals with me according to my righteousness and rewards
  me according to the cleanness of my hands - Psalm 18:20
I AM shows himself faithful to the faithful and blameless
  to the blameless - Psalm 18:25
I AM saves the humble and brings low those with
  haughty eyes - Psalm 18:27
I AM keeps my lamp burning and turns my darkness
  into light - Psalm 18:28
I AM, his way is perfect, his word flawless and a shield to

all who take refuge in him - Psalm 18:30
I AM arms me with strength and makes my way
  perfect - Psalm 18:32
I AM makes my feet like hinds feet enabling me to stand
  on the heights - Psalm 18:33
I AM trains my hands for battle - Psalm 18:34
I AM gives me his shield of victory, his right hand sustains
  me and he stoops down to make me great - Psalm 18:35
I AM broadens the path beneath me so my ankles do
  not turn - Psalm 18:36
I AM makes my enemies turn their backs in flight and I
  destroy my foes - Psalm 18:40
I AM LIVES! Praise be to my Rock! Exalted be God
  my Savior - Psalm 18:46
I AM shows unfailing kindness to his anointed - Psalm 18:50b
I am trusting in the name of the Lord my God,
  not in chariots or horses - Psalm 20:7
I am boasting in the name of the Lord our God - Psalm 20:7b
I am not in want - Psalm 23:1
I am fearing no evil, for you are with me - Psalm 23:4
I am comforted by your rod and your staff - Psalm 23:4c
I am kept safe, hidden and set high upon a rock - Psalm 27:5
I am seeking your face O Lord - Psalm 27:8
I am strong and taking heart as I wait for the Lord - Psalm 27:14

I am ascribing to the Lord glory and strength, the glory
  due his name - Psalm 29:1
I am ascribing to the Lord the glory due his name - Psalm 29:2a
I am worshipping the Lord in the splendor of his
  holiness - Psalm 29:2b
I am exalting the Lord for he lifted me out of the depths - Psalm 30:1
I am singing to the Lord and praising his holy name - Psalm 30:4
I am taking refuge in you O Lord - Psalm 31:1
I am committing my spirit into your hands, you have
  ransomed me O Lord, you are the God of truth - Psalm 31:5
I AM is my hiding place - Psalm 32:7a
I am protected from trouble - Psalm 32:7b

I am surrounded with songs of deliverance - Psalm 32:7c
I am instructed and taught in the way I should go - Psalm 32:8a
I AM counsels and watches over me - Psalm 32:8b
I AM surrounds me with loving-kindness as I trust
  in him - Psalm 32:10b
I am glad in the LORD and rejoicing - Psalm 32:11a
I am singing for joy in the LORD - Psalm 33:1a
I am giving thanks to the LORD and singing praises to
  him with instruments - Psalm 33:2
I am singing to him a new song - Psalm 33:3a
I AM does all his work in faithfulness - Psalm 33:4b
I AM loves righteousness and justice - Psalm 33:5a
I AM looks from heaven and can see all the sons
  of men - Psalm 33:13
I AM looks out from his dwelling place and sees all the
  inhabitants of the earth - Psalm 33:14
I AM fashions the hearts of us all and understands all
  our works - Psalm 33:15
I AM's eye is on those who fear him - Psalm 33:18a
I AM delivers my soul from death and keeps me alive
  in famine - Psalm 33:19
I am trusting in his holy name - Psalm 33:21
I am blessing the LORD at all times, his praise is continually
  in my mouth - Psalm 34:1
I AM answers me when I seek him - Psalm 34:4a
I am delivered from all my fears - Psalm 34:4b
I am saved out of all my troubles - Psalm 34:6b
I AM encamps around and rescues them that fear him - Psalm 34:7
I am tasting and seeing that the LORD is good - Psalm 34:8a
I am blessed as I take refuge in him - Psalm 34:8b
I am fearing the LORD and there is no want - Psalm 34:9
I am seeking the LORD and lack no good thing - Psalm 34:10b
I am keeping my tongue from evil and my lips from
  speaking lies - Psalm 34:13
I am turning from evil and doing good, I seek peace and
  pursue it - Psalm 34:14
I AM is near to the broken hearted and saves those who are

crushed in spirit - Psalm 34:18

I AM redeems the soul of his servants and none of them
who take refuge in him will be condemned - Psalm 34:22

I AM contends with those who contend with me - Psalm 35:1a

I AM fights against those who fight against me - Psalm 35:1b

I AM delights in the prosperity of his servants - Psalm 35:27c

I am declaring with my tongue your righteousness, I praise you
all day long - Psalm 35:28

I AM's loving-kindness extends to the heavens, his
faithfulness reaches to the skies - Psalm 36:5

I AM's righteousness is like the mighty mountains - Psalm 36:6a

I AM's judgments are like a great deep, you preserve man
and beast - Psalm 36:6b

I AM's loving kindness is precious - Psalm 36:7a

I AM gives us to drink from the river of his delights - Psalm 36:8b

I am trusting in the LORD and doing good, I am dwelling
in the land and cultivating faithfulness - Psalm 37:3

I am delighting myself in the Lord and he gives me the desires
of my heart - Psalm 37:4

I am committing my way to the LORD trusting in him that he
will do it - Psalm 37:5

I AM brings forth my righteousness as the light and judgment
as the noonday sun - Psalm 37:6

I am resting in the LORD and waiting patiently for him - Psalm 37:7a

I am ceasing from anger and forsaking wrath - Psalm 37:8a

I am not fretting as it only leads to evil - Psalm 37:8b

I am waiting for the LORD and will inherit the land - Psalm 37:9

I AM sustains the righteous - Psalm 37:17b

I am departing from evil and doing good so I will
abide with him forever - Psalm 37:27

I AM loves justice - Psalm 37:27a

I AM does not forsake his godly ones, they are preserved
forever - Psalm 37:27b

I AM brought me up out of the pit of destruction and the
miry clay - Psalm 40:2a

I AM set my feet upon a rock making my footsteps
firm - Psalm 40:2b

I AM put a new song in my mouth a song of praise
  to my God - Psalm 40:3a
I AM has opened my ears - Psalm 40:6b
I AM delivers in a day of trouble - Psalm 41:1
I AM protects and keeps us alive - Psalm 41:2a
I AM sustains me on the sickbed and restores my health - Psalm 41:3
I AM commands his loving-kindness in daytime and
  his song at night - Psalm 42:8a
I AM saves me from my adversaries and those who hate me
  he puts to shame - Psalm 44:7
I AM anoints me with the oil of joy - Psalm 45:7
I am the Kings daughter and glorious within - Psalm 45:13a
I AM is our refuge and strength a very present help
  in trouble - Psalm 46:1
I AM the Lord of hosts is with us, the God of Jacob is our
  stronghold - Psalm 46:7
I am clapping my hands and shouting to God with the
  voice of Joy - Psalm 47:1
I am singing praises to God, singing praises to our King,
  I am singing praise - Psalm 47:6
I AM is the King of all the earth - Psalm 47:7
I AM reigns over the nations and sits on his holy throne - Psalm 47:8
I AM is great and greatly to be praised - Psalm 48:1
I AM desires truth in our inner most being - Psalm 51:6a
I AM makes me to know wisdom in the hidden parts - Psalm 51:6b
I AM purifies me with hyssop so I shall be clean, whiter
  than snow - Psalm 51:7
I am like a green olive tree in the house of God - Psalm 52:8a
I am giving God thanks forever because he has done it - Psalm 52:9
I am casting my burden upon the LORD - Psalm 55:22a
I AM sustains me when I cast my burden upon him - Psalm 55:22b
I am singing of God's strength, joyfully singing of his
  loving-kindness - Psalm 59:16a
I AM has been my strong hold, a refuge in my day of
  distress - Psalm 59:16b
I AM recompenses men according to their work - Psalm 62:12b
I AM, you are my God, earnestly I seek you, my soul thirsts for you,

my flesh yearns for you in a dry and weary land - Psalm 63:1
I am blessing God as long as I live, I lift up my hands
  in his name - Psalm 63:4
I am satisfied in my soul as with marrow and fatness, my
  mouth offers up praises with joyful lips - Psalm 63:5
I AM visits the earth and cause it to overflow - Psalm 65:9a
I AM keeps us in life and does not allow our feet to slip - Psalm 66:9
I AM tries us and refines us as silver is refined - Psalm 66:10
I AM blesses us that all the ends of the earth may
  fear him - Psalm 67:7
I am dwelling in the shelter of the Most High - Psalm 91:1a
I am resting in the shadow of the Almighty - Psalm 91:1b
I am rescued and protected because I love and acknowledge
  the LORD - Psalm 91:14
I am anointed with fresh oil - Psalm 92:10b
I am blessing the LORD with my soul and all that is
  within me - Psalm 103:1
I am pardoned of all my iniquities and healed of all
  disease - Psalm 103:3
I am redeemed from the pit - Psalm 103:4a
I am crowned with love and compassion - Psalm 103:4b
I am satisfied with good things, so that my youth is renewed
  like the eagles - Psalm 103:5
I am not treated as my sins deserve - Psalm 103:10a
I am forgiven as far as the east is from the west - Psalm 103:12
I am hemmed in, behind and before, God's hand is
  upon me - Psalm 139:5
I am guided by God's hand - Psalm 139:10
I am fearfully and wonderfully made - Psalm 139:14
I AM trains me for war and battle - Psalm 144:1
I am praising the LORD and singing a new song - Psalm 149:1
I am praising his name with dancing - Psalm 149:3a
I AM takes pleasure in his people - Psalm 149:4a
I am praising the LORD in his sanctuary and in his
  mighty expanse - Psalm 150:1
I am praising him for his mighty deeds according to his
  excellent greatness - Psalm 150:2

I am praising him with trumpet sound, harp and lyre - Psalm 150:3
I am praising him with timbrel, dancing, instruments
  and pipes - Psalm 150:4
I am praising him with loud resounding cymbals - Psalm 150:5

I am binding kindness and truth on my neck and writing them
  on the tablet of my heart - Proverbs 3:3
I am trusting in the LORD with all my heart - Proverbs 3:5
I am in all my ways acknowledging him - Proverbs 3:6a
I am not wise in my own eyes, I fear the LORD and turn
  away from evil - Proverbs 3:7a
I am acquiring wisdom and understanding - Proverbs 4:5a
I am watching over my heart with all diligence - Proverbs 4:23a
I am trusting in the LORD and kept safe - Proverbs 29:25

I am increasing in wisdom - Ecclesiastes 1:16
I am given wisdom, knowledge and joy - Ecclesiastes 2:26
I am a part of a three cord strand - Ecclesiastes 4:12
I am not letting my words be hasty or my thoughts
  impulsive - Ecclesiastes 5:2a
I am letting my words be few - Ecclesiastes 5:2b
I am not letting my speech cause me to sin - Ecclesiastes 5:6
I am taking nothing from the fruit of my labor, naked I came,
  naked I go - Ecclesiastes 5:15
I am not remembering the years of my life because God
  keeps me occupied with the gladness of heart - Ecclesiastes 5:20
I am fearing God and keeping his commandments - Ecclesiastes 12:13

I am brought into the kings' chambers - Song of Solomon 1:4b
I am extolling your love more than wine - Song of Solomon 1:4d
I am altogether beautiful, not a blemish in me - Song of Solomon 4:7
I am my beloveds and my beloved is mine - Song of Solomon 6:3a
I am my beloveds and his desire is for me - Song of Solomon 7:10

I am washing myself and making myself clean, ceasing
  to do evil - Isaiah 1:16
I am learning to do good and seek justice - Isaiah 1:17a

I am reproving the ruthless, defending the orphan and
  pleading for the widow - Isaiah 1:17b
I am walking in the light of the Lord - Isaiah 2:5
I am his delightful plant - Isaiah 5:7
I am giving thanks to you O Lord, you turn your anger
  away from me and comfort me - Isaiah 12:1
I am trusting in the Lord and I am not afraid for he is
  my strength and my song, my salvation - Isaiah 12:2
I am joyously drawing water from the springs of
  salvation - Isaiah 12:3
I am giving thanks to the Lord and calling on his name
  and making known his deeds among the people - Isaiah 12:4
I am praising the Lord in song for he has done
  gloriously, excellent things - Isaiah 12:5
I am crying aloud and shouting for joy for great is the
  Holy One of Israel - Isaiah - 12:6
I AM is the Everlasting Rock - Isaiah 26:4
I AM's word will stand forever - Isaiah 40:8b
I am his servant, chosen and not rejected - Isaiah 41:9b
I am strengthened, helped and upheld by his righteous
  right hand - Isaiah 41:10
I am precious in his sight, honored and loved - Isaiah 42:4a
I am called in righteousness, he holds me by the hand and
  watches over me - Isaiah 42:6
I AM makes crooked things straight - Isaiah 42:16d
I am created, called and redeemed me, I am his - Isaiah 43:1
I AM is with me when I pass through the waters - Isaiah 43:2a
I am not swept over when I pass through the rivers - Isaiah 43:2b
I am not burned when I walk through the fire - Isaiah 43:2c
I AM is the Holy One of Israel, my Savior - Isaiah 43:3
I am chosen as his servant - Isaiah 43:10a
I AM is the LORD, there is no savior besides him - Isaiah 43:11
I AM He - Isaiah 43:13a
I AM acts and who can reverse it? - Isaiah 43:13c
I AM the LORD is my Redeemer, the Holy One of
  Israel - Isaiah 43:14
I AM is the LORD, the Holy One, the Creator of Israel,

my King - Isaiah 43:15

I AM blots out transgressions and remembers our sins
no more - Isaiah 43:25

I AM chose me - Isaiah 44:1

I AM made and formed me in the womb - Isaiah 44:2

I AM is the first and the last - Isaiah 44:6b

I AM, the LORD, makes all things - Isaiah 44:24

I AM will not give his glory to another - Isaiah 48:11c

I AM is the first and he is the last - Isaiah 48:12b

I AM laid the foundation of the world - Isaiah 48:13

I AM hides me in the shadow of his hand - Isaiah 49:2b

I am given an instructed tongue, to know the word that
sustains the weary - Isaiah 50:4a

I am covered with the shadow of his hand - Isaiah 51:16b

I am healed by his wounds - Isaiah 53:5d

I AM is the LORD of hosts, the Holy One of Israel, my redeemer,
the God of the whole earth - Isaiah 54:5

I am refuting every tongue that accuses me - Isaiah 54:17b

I am vindicated by the LORD - Isaiah 54:17c

I am endowed with splendor - Isaiah 55:5c

I am abundantly pardoned - Isaiah 55:7c

I am going out in joy and being led forth by peace - Isaiah 55:12a

I am maintaining justice and doing what is right - Isaiah 56:1a

I am given an everlasting name which will not be
cut off - Isaiah 56:5b

I AM is the mighty one of Jacob - Isaiah 60:16d

I am anointed to preach good news - Isaiah 61:1a

I am sent to bind up the broken hearted - Isaiah 61:1b

I am proclaiming liberty to the captives and freedom to
the prisoners - Isaiah 61:1c

I am proclaiming the favorable year of the Lord and the
day of vengeance - Isaiah 61:2a

I am comforting all who mourn and I give to them a garland,
oil and a mantle of praise - Isaiah 61:2b-3

I am called a priest of the Lord and a minister of God who
eats the wealth of nations - Isaiah 61:6

I am given a double portion and everlasting joy shall

be mine - Isaiah 61:7
I am rejoicing greatly in the Lord, my soul exults in
my God - Isaiah 61:10a
I am clothed with garments of salvation and wrapped
in a robe of righteousness - Isaiah 61:10b
I am a crown of splendor in the hand of the LORD, a royal
diadem in God's hand - Isaiah 62:3

I AM is watching over his word to perform it - Jeremiah 1:12b
I AM knew me before he formed me in my mother's
womb - Jeremiah 1:5a
I am consecrated and approved by the Lord - Jeremiah 1:5b
I AM is with me to deliver me - Jeremiah 1:8
I AM has put his words in my mouth - Jeremiah 1:9
I am appointed over nations and kingdoms - Jeremiah 1:10
I AM watches over his word to see that it is fulfilled - Jeremiah 1:12
I am made as a fortified city, a pillar of iron and walls
of bronze - Jeremiah 1:18
I AM is with me and will rescue me - Jeremiah 1:19a
I am not overcome because I AM is with me to deliver
me - Jeremiah 1:19b
I AM brings us into a fertile land to eat its fruit and
rich produce - Jeremiah 2:7
I AM is the spring of living water - Jeremiah 2:13
I am corrected by my own wickedness and reproved by my
own apostasies - Jeremiah 2:19a
I AM is gracious and merciful - Jeremiah 3:12d
I AM will not be angry forever - Jeremiah 3:12e
I am acknowledging my iniquity and transgression against
the Lord - Jeremiah 3:13
I AM is my Master - Jeremiah 3:14b
I AM will give me a shepherd after his own heart to feed me
on knowledge and understanding - Jeremiah 3:15a
I AM will heal my faithlessness when I return to him - Jeremiah 3:22
I am breaking up the fallow ground - Jeremiah 4:3a
I am not sowing among thorns - Jeremiah 4:3b
I am circumcising myself to the Lord - Jeremiah 4:4a

I am removing the foreskin of my heart - Jeremiah 4:4b
I am washing my heart from evil that I may be saved - Jeremiah 4:14a
I am mending my ways and deeds - Jeremiah 7:3
I am obeying his voice and walking in the way he commands so
  that it may be well with me - Jeremiah 7:23
I am boasting this, that I know and understand the
  Lord - Jeremiah 9:24a
I AM exercises loving-kindness, justice and righteousness on
  the earth, in these he delights - Jeremiah 9:24b
I am not learning the way of nations nor am I terrified by the
  signs of heaven - Jeremiah 10:2
I am cursed if I do not heed the words of this
  covenant - Jeremiah 11:3
I am listening to his voice and doing all he
  commands - Jeremiah 11:4b
I AM, the Lord of hosts, judges righteously, he tries the
  feelings and the heart - Jeremiah 11:20
I am restored when I return to the Lord - Jeremiah 15:19a
I am extracting the precious from the worthless - Jeremiah 15:19b
I am delivered from the wicked and redeemed from the
  grasp of the violent - Jeremiah 15:21

I AM saves me from the hands of the wicked and redeems
  me from the grasp of the cruel - Jeremiah 15:23
I AM the Lord is my strength and my stronghold, my refuge
  in the day of distress - Jeremiah 16:19a
I am blessed as I trust in the Lord - Jeremiah 17:7
I am like a tree planted by the water - Jeremiah 17:8a
I AM gives to each man according to his ways, according
  to the results of his deeds - Jeremiah 17:10b
I am keeping the Sabbath day holy - 17:22b
I am turning back from my evil ways, I am reforming my
  ways and deeds - Jeremiah 18:11b
I AM rescues the life of the needy from the hands of the
  wicked - Jeremiah 20:13b
I am doing justice, righteousness and delivering the one who has
  been robbed from the power of his oppressor - Jeremiah 22:3a

I am not mistreating or being violent to the stranger, orphans
  or widows - Jeremiah 22:3b
I am not shedding innocent blood - Jeremiah 22:3b
I AM is the Lord our righteousness - Jeremiah 23:6c
I AM fills the heavens and the earth - Jeremiah 23:24b
I am speaking his word in truth - Jeremiah 23:28b
I am turning from evil ways and deeds - Jeremiah 25:5
I am not going after other gods to serve and worship
  them - Jeremiah 25:6a
I am not provoking the Lord to anger with the works of
  my hands - Jeremiah 25: 6b
I AM knows the plans he has for me, plans to prosper me and not
  to harm me, plans to give me a future and a hope - Jeremiah 29:11
I AM disciplines, but only with justice - Jeremiah 30:11c
I AM restores me to health and heals all my
  wounds - Jeremiah 30:17a
I am loved with an everlasting love - Jeremiah 31:3b
I am made to walk by streams of water on a straight path
  and without stumbling I am led - Jeremiah 31:9
I am ransomed and redeemed from a hand stronger
  than I - Jeremiah 31:11
I am comforted and given joy for my sorrow - Jeremiah 31:13c
I AM satisfies the weary ones and refreshes everyone
  who languishes - Jeremiah 31:25
I am forgiven of my iniquity and he remembers my
  sin no more - Jeremiah 31:34c
I am given to according to my ways and the fruit of
  my deeds - Jeremiah 32:19b
I AM the LORD is the God of all mankind, there is nothing
  to hard for him - Jeremiah 32:27
I am made to dwell in safety - Jeremiah 32:37
I am given one heart and one way that I may fear
  God always - Jeremiah 32:39a
I AM invites me to call to him, he will answer and tell me great
  and mighty things that I do not know - Jeremiah 33:3
I AM brings health and healing and reveals an abundance
  of peace and truth - Jeremiah 33:6

I am turning from my evil ways and amending them - Jeremiah 35:15

I am not consumed because his compassions fail
  not - Lamentations 3:22

I am prophesying to dry bones! - Ezekiel 37:1-5

I am silent before the Lord - Zephaniah 1:7

I AM's name will be great among the nations - Malachi 1:11
I AM is a great king and his name is feared among
  the nations - Malachi 1:14b
I am preserving knowledge - Malachi 2:7a
I am purified like gold and silver - Malachi 3:3b
I am his; he spares me as a son - Malachi 3:17
I am going forth skipping like a calf from the stall - Malachi 4:2b
I am treading down the wicked; they will be ashes under
  the soles of my feet - Malachi 4:3

The New Testament

I AM will save his people from their sins - Matthew 1:21
I AM is our Shepherd - Matthew 2:6b
I AM was given gifts of gold, frankincense and myrrh - Matthew 2:11
I AM clears the threshing floor and burns up the chaff - Matthew 3:12
I AM was baptized - Matthew 3:16a
I AM descended from the heavens like a dove - Matthew 3:16b
I AM is my beloved Son in whom I am well pleased - Matthew 3:17
I AM will command his angels concerning us - Matthew 4:6
I AM is ministered to by angels - Matthew 4:11
I am a fisher of men - Matthew 4:19
I AM blesses the poor in spirit - Matthew 5:3
I AM blesses those who mourn - Matthew 5:4
I AM blesses the gentle - Matthew 5:5
I AM blesses those who thirst and hunger for
  righteousness - Matthew 5:6

I AM blesses the merciful - Matthew 5:7
I AM blesses the pure in heart - Matthew 5:8
I AM blesses the peacemakers - Matthew 5:9
I AM blesses those who have been persecuted - Matthew 5:10
I AM blesses us when we are insulted because
  of him - Matthew 5:11
I am the salt and light of the earth - Matthew 5:13
I am the light of the world - Matthew 5:14
I AM rewards your giving in secret - Matthew 6:4
I AM forgives us when we forgive others - Matthew 6:14
I AM sees what is done in secret - Matthew 6:18
I am rewarded for fasting in secret - Matthew 6:18b
I am not worrying about tomorrow - Matthew 6:34
I AM feeds the birds of the air - Matthew 6:26
I am much more valuable than the birds of the air that
  my Father in heaven feeds - Matthew 6:26
I AM knows all that we need - Matthew 6:32
I AM knows how to give good gifts to those that ask - Matthew 7:11
I AM teaches with authority - Matthew 7:28
I AM is willing to touch and heal - Matthew 8:3
I AM casts out spirits with a word and heals - Matthew 8:16
I AM himself took up our infirmities and carried away
  our infirmities - Matthew 8:17
I AM rebuked the wind and the waves and they became
  calm - Matthew 8:26
I am given authority to drive out evil spirits and to heal
  every disease and sickness - Matthew 10:1
I am preaching, healing, raising the dead and driving
  out demons - Matthew 10:7
I am shrewd as a serpent and innocent as a dove - Matthew 10:16
I am loved so individually that he has even counted the
  hairs on my head - Matthew 10:30
I AM gives rest to those who come to him when they
  are weary - Matthew 11:28
I AM says: Take courage! It is I. Do not be afraid - Matthew 14:27b
I AM builds his church - Matthew 16:18
I AM says that if we have faith as small as a mustard seed we

can move mountains - Matthew 17:20

I AM desires that none should perish - Matthew 18:14

I AM healed in large crowds - Matthew 19:2

I AM says with God all things are possible - Matthew 19:26

I AM is generous - Matthew 20:15

I AM came to serve and give his life as a ransom for
many - Matthew 20:28

I AM, our King, came to us gentle and mounted on a
donkey - Matthew 21:5

I AM gives all things that we ask for in prayer when we
believe - Matthew 21:22

I AM is not the God of the dead but the God of the
living - Matthew 22:32

I AM's words will never pass away - Matthew 24:35

I am going and making disciples of all nations - Matthew 28:19

I AM is with me always even unto the end of the age - Matthew 28:20

I AM will make us fishers of men when we follow him - Mark 1:17

I AM preaches and casts out demons - Mark 1:39

I AM cleanses leprosy - Mark 1:42

I AM is the LORD of the Sabbath - Mark 2:28

I AM gives and I AM takes away - Mark 4:25

I AM rebukes the wind and it obeys - Mark 4:39

I AM says to him who believes, all things are possible - Mark 9:23

I AM declares that when we give up things for his sake we
will receive 100 fold in return - Mark 10:30

I AM will be seen coming in the clouds with great power
and glory - Mark 13:26

I AM's words will never pass a way - Mark 13:31

I am placing my hands on sick people and they do
get well - Mark 16:18

I AM will reign over the house of Jacob forever and his
kingdom shall have no end - Luke 1:33

I AM has done great things for me - Luke 1:49

I AM's name is Holy - Luke 1:49b

I AM's mercy is upon generation after generation to those

who fear him - Luke 1:50

I AM has done mighty deeds with his arm - Luke 1:51

I AM brought rulers down from their thrones - Luke 1:52

I AM exalts those who are humble - Luke 1:52b

I AM fills the hungry with good things - Luke 1:53

I AM has accomplished redemption for his people - Luke 1:68b

I AM has raised up a horn of salvation - Luke 1:69

I AM saves us from our enemies and all who hate us - Luke 1:71

I AM is merciful to our ancestors - Luke 1:72

I AM rescued us from our enemies so we can serve God
   without fear - Luke 1:74

I AM's mercy is tender - Luke 1:78

I AM is called "The Sunrise from on high" who visits us - Luke 1:78b

I AM will shine upon those who sit in darkness - Luke 1:79

I AM will guide our feet into the way of peace - Luke 1:79b

I AM grew and became strong - Luke 2:40

I am anointed to preach the good news to the poor - Luke 4:18

I am given authority to trample on snakes and scorpions - Luke 10:19

I am given authority to overcome all the power of
   the enemy - Luke 10:19

I am endued with power from on high - Luke 24:49

I am a child of God - John 1:12

I AM appoints each persons work - John 3:27

I AM comes from above and is greater than anyone else - John 3:31

I AM has the gift of living water for those who ask - John 4:10

I AM, Messiah - John 4:26

I AM never stops working - John 5:17

I am a possessor of eternal life - John 5:24

I AM walks on water - John 6:19

I AM the true bread comes down from heaven and gives
   life to the world - John 6:33

I AM is the bread of life - John 6:35

I am is a gift to Jesus from God himself and he will not
   cast me out - John 6:37

I AM raises us from the dead - John 6:44

I am promised eternal life - John 6:47

I AM is the living bread that came down from heaven - John 6:51
I AM has the words that give eternal life - John 6:68
I AM accuses the world of sin and evil - John 7:7
I AM is the light of the world - John 8:12
I AM knows where he came from and where he is going - John 8:14
I AM is the one he always claimed to be - John 8:25
I am truly a disciple of Christ - John 8:31
I am his disciple as I continue in his word - John 8:31
I am knowing and set free by the truth - John 8:32
I am Abraham's descendant - John 8:33
I AM, the Son, is who sets us free - John 8:36
I am preaching that the kingdom of heaven is at hand - John 10:7
I am healing the sick, raising the dead, cleansing the
  leper and casting out demons - John 10:8
I AM is the gate - John 10:9
I AM's purpose is to give life in all its fullness - John 10:10
I AM knows me - John 10:27
I AM gives eternal life - John 10:28
I am an inheritor of eternal life, I will never perish and no
  one can snatch me out of his hand - John 10:28
I AM is one with the Father - John 10:30
I AM is the resurrection and the Life - John 11:25
I AM goes to prepare a place for me - John 14:2
I am at home in him - John 14:23
I AM is the way, the truth and the life and no one comes to
  the Father but through him - John 14:6
I AM's words are not his own, but his Father who lives
  in him - John 14:10
I AM will ask the Father to give us another counselor - John 14:16
I AM will not abandon us or leave us as orphans - John 14:18
I AM gives us peace of mind and heart as a gift - John 14:27
I AM is the true vine! - John 15:1
I am a branch of the true vine - John 15:1
I am clean because of the word Jesus has spoken to me - John 15:3
I am is the vine and we are the branches - John 15:5
I am Christ's friend - John 15:15
I AM, chose me - John 15:16a

I am chosen and appointed to bear fruit - John 15:16
I AM appointed me to go and produce fruit that
  will last - John 15:16b
I AM commands us to love each other - John 15:17
I AM has overcome the world - John 16:33
I AM is the only way to have eternal life - John 17:3a
I AM is the one sent to earth - John 17:3b
I AM is ready to go the Father - John 17:13
I AM he, Jesus of Nazareth - John 18:5
I AM shall drink from the cup the Father has given him - John18:11
I AM is not an earthly king - John 1836a
I AM's Kingdom is not of this world - John 18:36b
I AM was frying fish - John 21:9
I AM extends invitations - John 21:12
I AM served the bread and fish - John 21:13
I AM says: "Follow me"- John 21:19

I am a personal witness of Christ's - Acts 1:8
I am endued with power from on high - Acts 2:4
I am baptized with the Holy Spirit - Acts 11:16c
I AM is with me so no man will attack or hurt me - Acts 18:10a

I am set apart for the gospel of God - Romans 1:1
I am the called of Jesus Christ - Romans 1:6
I am serving God in my spirit as I preach the gospel - Romans1:9
I am encouraged by others faith - Romans 1:12
I am living by faith - Romans 1:17
I am inwardly a Jew - Romans 2:29
I am circumcised by the spirit - Romans 2:29
I am justified freely by his grace - Romans 3:24a
I am justified by faith apart from works of the law - Romans 3:28
I am calling things that be not as though they are - Romans 4:17
I am not wavering in unbelief, but growing strong in
  faith giving glory to God - Romans 4:20
I am fully assured that what God has promised, he is able
  to do - Romans 4:21
I am at peace with God having been justified by faith through

our Lord Jesus Christ - Romans 5:1

I am exulting in my tribulations bringing about perseverance,
proven character and hope - Romans 5:3-4

I am justified by his blood - Romans 5:9a

I am saved from the wrath of God through Jesus - Romans 5:9b

I am reconciled to God through the death of his Son - Romans 5:10a

I am reigning in life through the One, Jesus Christ - Romans 5:17b

I am dead to sin - Romans 6:2

I am buried with him through baptism into death, so I might
walk in newness of life - Romans 6:4

I am united with him in his death, so I can be united with him
in his resurrection - Romans 6:5

I am no longer a slave to sin - Romans 6:6b

I am dead to sin but alive to God in Christ Jesus - Romans 6:11

I am not letting sin reign in my mortal body so that I obey
its lust - Romans 6:12

I am presenting myself to God as one alive from the dead and
my members as instruments of righteousness - Romans 6:13b

I am not under law, but under grace - Romans 6:14

I am freed from sin and have become a slave to
righteousness - Romans 6:18

I am freed from sin and enslaved to God resulting in
sanctification - Romans 6:22

I am released from the law, so I may serve in newness
of the Spirit, not oldness of the letter - Romans 7:6

I am free forever from condemnation - Romans 8:1

I am set free from the law of sin and death - Romans 8:2

I am setting my mind on the things of the Spirit
{life and peace} - Romans 8:6

I am not in the flesh, but in the Spirit, the Spirit of God
dwells in me - Romans 8:9a

I am given life in my mortal body through his Spirit who
lives in me - Romans 8:11

I am not obligated to do as my sinful nature urges
me to - Romans 8:12

I am led by the Spirit of God - Romans 8:13

I am being led by the Spirit of God - Romans 8:14

I am adopted as a son and cry out, Abba Father! - Romans 8:15
I am a child of God - Romans 8:16
I am an heir of God and a fellow heir with Christ - Romans 8:17a
I am suffering with him so I may also be glorified with
  him - Romans 8:17b
I am eagerly awaiting my adoption, the redemption of
  my body - Romans 8:23
I am with hope waiting eagerly for what I do not
  yet see - Romans 8:25
I am helped in my weakness by the Spirit who intercedes
  for me - Romans 8:26
I am assured that all things work together for good to those
  who love God - Romans 8:28a
I am called according to his purpose - Romans 8:28b
I am predestined to be conformed to the image of
  his Son - Romans 8:29a
I am predestined, called, justified and glorified - Romans 8:30a
I am free from any condemning charges against me - Romans 8:33
I am more than a conqueror through Christ - Romans 8:37
I am convinced that nothing will be able to separate me
  from the love of God - Romans 8:38
I am a child of the promise, regarded as a descendant - Romans 9:8b
I am believing in him and will not be disappointed - Romans 9:33b
I am grafted in among them and a partaker with them of
  the rich root of the olive tree - Romans 11:17
I am supported by the root - Romans 11:18b
I am presenting my body as a living sacrifice, acceptable
  to God - Romans 12:1b
I am not conformed to this world - Romans 12:2a
I am transformed by the renewing of my mind - Romans 12:2a
I am not thinking more highly of myself than I ought - Romans 12:3a
I am allotted a measure of faith - Romans 12:3b
I am exercising the gifts given me according to the grace given
  me - Romans 12:6 {prophecy-serving-teaching-exhortation-
  giving-leading-mercy}
I am clinging to what is good - Romans 12:9b
I am devoted to others in brotherly love, giving preference

to them - Romans 12:10

I am not lagging behind, but fervent in Spirit, serving
the Lord - Romans 12:11

I am rejoicing in hope, persevering in tribulation, devoted
to prayer - Romans 12:12

I am contributing to the needs of the saints and practicing
hospitality - Romans 12:13

I am blessing those who persecute me - Romans 12:14

I am rejoicing with those who rejoice and I weep with
those who weep - Romans 12:15

I am of the same mind toward others - Romans 12:16a

I am not haughty but associate with the lowly - Romans 12:16b

I am not wise in my own estimation - Romans 12:16c

I am respecting what is right in the sight of all men - Romans 12:17b

I am at peace with all men - Romans 12:18

I am not overcome by evil, rather, I overcome evil with
good - Romans 12:21

I am in subjection to the governing authorities - Romans 13:1

I am rendering to all what is due them - Romans 13:7a

I am loving my neighbor as myself - Romans 13:9b

I am laying aside the deeds of darkness and putting on the
armor of light - Romans 13:12b

I am putting on the Lord Jesus Christ - Romans 13:14a

I am making no provision for the flesh in regard to
lust - Romans 13:14b

I am accepting those who are week in faith - Romans 14:1

I am living for the Lord, I am his - Romans 14:8

I am not putting obstacles or stumbling blocks in a
brother's way - Romans14:13b

I am pursuing the things which make for peace and the
building up of one another - Romans 14:19

I am pleasing my neighbor for his own good and
edification - Romans 15:2

I am waiting patiently for God's promises - Romans 15:4b

I am in one accord, with one voice, glorifying God the
Father of our Lord Jesus Christ - Romans 15:6

I am accepting others just as Christ accepted me to the

glory of God - Romans 15:7
I am filled with all joy and peace, as I trust in him, so I overflow
  with hope by the power of the Holy Spirit - Romans 15:13
I am a minister of the gospel of God - Romans 15:16
I am wise in what is good and innocent in what
  is evil - Romans 16:19b

I am sanctified in him - 1 Corinthians 1:2
I am given grace in him - 1 Corinthians 1:4
I am enriched in every way through Christ - 1 Corinthians 1:5
I am God's fellow worker, I am God's field and I am
  God's building - 1 Corinthians 3:9
I am a temple of God and his Spirit lives in me - 1 Corinthians 3:16
I am a servant of Christ - 1 Corinthians 4:1a
I am a steward of the mysteries of God - 1 Corinthians 4:1b
I am examined by the Lord - 1 Corinthians 4:4
I am blessing when reviled and enduring when
  persecuted - 1 Corinthians 4:12
I am united with the Lord and one with him in
  spirit - 1 Corinthians 6:17
I am not my own I was bought with a price - 1 Corinthians 6:19
I am a temple of the Holy Spirit - 1 Corinthians 6:19
I am called by God - 1 Corinthians 7:17
I am a member of Christ's body - 1 Corinthians 12:27
I am being shown the most excellent way - 1 Corinthians 13:1a
I AM is patient, kind, not jealous, doesn't brag, is not arrogant,
  does not act unbecomingly, doesn't seek his own, in not provoked,
  does not take into account wrongs suffered, does not rejoice
  in unrighteousness but rejoices with the truth - 1 Corinthians 13:4-6
I AM bears all things, believes all things, hopes all things and
  endures all things. 1 Corinthians 13:7
I AM never fails - 1 Corinthians 13:8a
I am victorious through Jesus Christ - 1 Corinthians 15:57

I am established, anointed and sealed by God - 2 Corinthians 1:21
I am led by God in triumphal procession - 2 Corinthians 2:14
I am to God the aroma of Christ to those being saved and to

those who are perishing - 2 Corinthians 2:15
I am not adequate in myself, my adequacy comes from
God - 2 Corinthians 3:5
I am being transformed into his likeness with ever-increasing
glory - 2 Corinthians 3:18
I am being inwardly renewed day by day - 2 Corinthians 4:16
I am fixing my eyes on what is unseen - 2 Corinthians 4:18
I am no longer living for myself but for him who died for
me and rose again - 2 Corinthians 5:15
I am a new creation, the old is gone the new is
come - 2 Corinthians 5:17
I am reconciled to God through Christ - 2 Corinthians 5:18
I am a minister of reconciliation - 2 Corinthians 5:18
I am an ambassador for Christ - 2 Corinthians 5:20
I am the righteousness of God because Jesus became
sin for me - 2 Corinthians 5:21
I am God's co-worker - 2 Corinthians 6:1
I am not bound together with unbelievers - 2 Corinthians 6:14
I am the temple of the living God - 2 Corinthians 6:16b
I am given divine power to demolish strongholds - 2 Corinthians 10:4
I am destroying speculations and every lofty thing that raises
itself up against the knowledge of God - 2 Corinthians 10:5a
I am taking every thought captive and making it obedient
to Christ - 2 Corinthians 10:5b
I am given strength for my weakness - 2 Corinthians 12:10

I am crucified with Christ and I no longer live, but Christ
lives in me - Galatians 2:20
I am redeemed from the curse of the law - Galatians 3:13
I am a son of God through Jesus Christ - Galatians 3:26
I am Abraham's seed... an heir to promise - Galatians 3:29
I am no longer a slave but a son, and an heir - Galatians 4:7

I am a saint - Ephesians 1:1a
I am faithful - Ephesians 1:1b
I am blessed with every spiritual blessing in Christ - Ephesians 1:3
I am chosen from before the foundation of the world - Ephesians 1:4a

I am holy and blameless before him - Ephesians 1:4b
I am predestined to be adopted as God's child - Ephesians 1:5
I am freely given his grace - Ephesians 1:6
I am redeemed forgiven of my sin - Ephesians 1:7
I am a recipient of his lavish grace - Ephesians 1:8
I AM reveals his will to me - Ephesians 1:9
I am given an inheritance - Ephesians 1:11a
I am sealed in him with the Holy Spirit of promise - Ephesians 1:11b
I am sealed in him with the Holy Spirit of promise - Ephesians 1:13
I am given the Holy Spirit as a pledge of my
  inheritance - Ephesians 1:14
I am loved by God - Ephesians 2:4
I am made alive together with Christ - Ephesians 2:5
I am raised up with him, and seated with him in the
  heavenly places - Ephesians 2:6
I am saved by grace - Ephesians 2:8
I am his workmanship, created in Christ Jesus - Ephesians 2:10a
I am walking in the good works which God created
  for me - Ephesians 2:10b
I am no longer separated from Christ - Ephesians 2:12
I am brought near by the blood of the lamb - Ephesians 2:13
I AM himself is our peace - Ephesians 2:14
I am granted access to the Father through Christ - Ephesians 2:18
I am no longer a stranger, but a fellow citizen - Ephesians 2:19a
I am a member of God's household - Ephesians 2:19b
I am of God's household - Ephesians 2:19c
I am built upon the foundation of the apostles and
  prophets - Ephesians 2:20
I am growing into a holy temple of the Lord - Ephesians 2:21
I am being built together into a dwelling of God in
  the Spirit - Ephesians 2:22
I am made a minister according to the grace given me - Ephesians 3:7
I am given boldness and confident access through faith
  in him - Ephesians 3:12
I am strengthened with power thought his spirit in my
  inner man - Ephesians 3:16
I am able to comprehend with all the saints, the breadth, length,

height and depth of the love of Christ - Ephesians 3:18-19a
I am filled up to all the fullness of God - Ephesians 3:19b
I am walking in a manner worthy of the calling I have
  received - Ephesians 4:1
I am humble, gentle and patient showing tolerance for
  others in love - Ephesians 4:3
I am called in one hope, one Lord, one faith, one baptism,
  one God and Father of all - Ephesians 4:4-6
I am given grace according to the measure of Christ's
  gift - Ephesians 4:7
I am equipped for the work of service to build up
  the body - Ephesians 4:12
I am attaining to the full measure of Christ - Ephesians 4:13
I am no longer a child, tossed here and there by waves and
  carried about by every wind of doctrine, by the trickery of
  men, or by the craftiness in deceitful scheming - Ephesians 4:14
I am speaking the truth in love and growing up in all aspects
  into him - Ephesians 4:15
I am being fitted and held together by what every joint
  supplies - Ephesians 4:16
I am no longer walking like the gentiles in futility
  of mind - Ephesians 4:17
I am laying aside the old self - Ephesians 4:22
I am being renewed in the spirit of my mind - Ephesians 4:23
I am putting on the new self, the likeness of God - Ephesians 4:24a
I am created in righteousness, holiness and truth - Ephesians 4:24b
I am laying aside falsehood and speaking the truth to
  others - Ephesians 4:25
I am not sinning in my anger - Ephesians 4:26
I am not giving the devil an opportunity - Ephesians 4:27
I am laboring and performing with my own hands what
  is good - Ephesians 4:28
I am letting no unwholesome talk proceed out of my mouth, but
  only words as are good for edification according to the need at
  the moment giving grace to the hearer - Ephesians 4:29
I am not grieving the Holy Spirit - Ephesians 4:30
I am letting all bitterness, wrath, anger, clamor, slander and

malice be put away from me - Ephesians 4:31

I am kind, tender hearted and forgiving towards others just
as Christ has been to me - Ephesians 4:32

I am an imitator of God and beloved - Ephesians 5:1

I am walking in love - Ephesians 5:2

I am not immoral, impure or greedy - Ephesians 5:3

I am not talking filthy, coarsely, silly or jesting,
instead I am giving thanks - Ephesians 5:4

I am not deceived with or by empty words - Ephesians 5:6

I am light in the Lord - Ephesians 5:8

I am learning what is pleasing to the Lord - Ephesians 5:10

I am not participating in the unfruitful deeds of darkness;
rather I am exposing them - Ephesians 5:11

I am not speaking of things done in secret - Ephesians 5:12

I am careful how I walk, not as unwise, but as wise - Ephesians 5:15

I am making the most of my time - Ephesians 5; 16

I am not foolish, but understand what the will of the
Lord is - Ephesians 5:17

I am not getting drunk on wine; rather I am being filled
with the Spirit - Ephesians 5:18

I am speaking to others in psalms, hymns and spiritual songs
making melody in my heart to God - Ephesians 5:19

I am giving thanks for all things in the name of our Lord
Jesus Christ - Ephesians 5:20

I am subject to others in the fear of Christ - Ephesians 5:21

I am subject to my own husband, as to the Lord - Ephesians 5:22

I am sanctified and cleansed by the word - Ephesians 5:26

I am presented by Jesus with no spot or wrinkle, in him I am
holy and blameless - Ephesians 5:27

I am loved by my husband as he loves his own body - Ephesians5:28

I am nourished and cared for by Christ - Ephesians 5:29b

I am a member of his body - Ephesians 5:30

I am one flesh with my husband - Ephesians 5:31

I am respecting my husband - Ephesians 5:33

I am obeying my parents - Ephesians 6:1

I am honoring my father and mother that I may be well
and live long on the earth - Ephesians 6:2-3

I am not provoking my children to anger, but bringing them up
  in the discipline and instruction of the Lord - Ephesians 6:4
I am obedient to my masters as to Christ - Ephesians 6:5
I am doing the will of God from my heart - Ephesians 6:6
I am with good will rendering service as to the Lord and not
  to men - Ephesians 6:7
I am receiving back from the Lord whatever good
  thing I do - Ephesians 6:8
I am strong in the mighty strength of the Lord - Ephesians 6:10
I am putting on the full armor of God and standing firm
  against the devil's schemes - Ephesians 6:11
I am struggling against the rulers, powers, world forces of
  darkness and the spiritual forces of wickedness - Ephesians 6:12
I am putting on the full armor of God to be able to resist in
  the evil day - Ephesians 6:13
I am standing firm having girded my loins with truth, I
  have put on the breastplate of righteousness - Ephesians 6:14
I am shodding my feet with the preparation of the
  gospel of peace - Ephesians 6:15
I am taking up the shield of faith so I may extinguish all the
  flaming arrows of the evil one - Ephesians 6:17
I am praying and asking at all times in the Spirit - Ephesians 6:18a
I am alert and persevering for all the saints - Ephesians 6:18b
I am praying with boldness that utterance be given me to
  make known the mystery of the gospel - Ephesians 6:19
I am an ambassador and I am speaking boldly
  as I ought - Ephesians 6:20
I am receiving comfort for my heart by beloved brothers
  and faithful ministers of Christ - Ephesians 6:21-22
I am given peace, love and faith from God the Father and the
  Lord Jesus Christ - Ephesians 6:23

I am thanking God in remembrance of others - Philippians 1:3
I am offering prayer with joy for others - Philippians 1:4
I am confident that he who began a good work in me will
  perfect it - Philippians 1:6
I am a partaker of grace - Philippians 1:7b

I am praying that your love may abound more and more in
  real knowledge and discernment - Philippians 1:9
I am approving the things that are excellent so I am sincere
  and blameless - Philippians 1:10
I am filled with the fruit of righteousness through Jesus
  Christ - Philippians 1:11
I am preaching Christ through good will - Philippians 1:15
I am proclaiming Christ in truth and in this I rejoice - Philippians 1:18
I am not put to shame in anything - Philippians 1:20
I am living for Christ and to die is gain - Philippians 1:21
I am conducting myself in a manner worthy of the
  gospel - Philippians 1:27a
I am standing firm in one spirit with my mind striving for the
  faith of the gospel - Philippians 1:27b
I am not alarmed by my opponents - Philippians 1:28
I am believing in him, but also suffer for his sake - Philippians 1:29
I am encouraged in Christ, consoled in love and fellowship
  with the Spirit - Philippians 2:1
I am maintaining love, united in spirit and intent on one
  purpose - Philippians 2:2
I am not doing anything from selfish or empty
  conceit - Philippians 2:3a
I am with humility of mind regarding others as more
  important than myself - Philippians 2:3b
I am looking out for the interest of others - Philippians 2:4
I am emptying myself and taking on the form of a bond
  servant - Philippians 2:7
I am confessing that Jesus Christ is Lord to the glory of
  God the Father - Philippians 2:11
I am working out my salvation with fear and
  trembling - Philippians 2:12
I am doing all things without grumbling or
  disputing - Philippians 2:14
I am proving myself to be a blameless and innocent child of
  God, above reproach - Philippians 2:15a
I am in the midst of a crooked and perverse generation appearing
  as a light in the world - Philippians 2:15b

I am holding fast to the word of life - Philippians 2:16a
I am not running or toiling in vain - Philippians 2:16b
I am rejoicing and sharing my joy - Philippians 2:18
I am rejoicing in the Lord - Philippians 3:1
I am aware of the dogs, the evil workers and the false
  circumcision - Philippians 3:2
I am the true circumcision, I worship in the Spirit of God
  and glory in Christ Jesus - Philippians 3:3a
I am putting no confidence in the flesh - Philippians 3:3b
I am counting all things as loss in view of the surpassing
  value of knowing Christ Jesus, my Lord - Philippians 3:8
I am being conformed to his death in order that I may attain to
  the resurrection of the dead - Philippians 3:10b-11
I am pressing on so I may lay hold of that for which I was laid
  hold of by Christ Jesus - Philippians 3:12
I am forgetting what lies behind and reaching forward to
  what lies ahead - Philippians 3:13
I am pressing on toward the goal for the prize of the upward
  call of God in Christ Jesus - Philippians 3:14
I am living by the same standard to which I have
  attained - Philippians 3:16
I am eagerly awaiting the Savior, the Lord Jesus
  Christ - Philippians 3:20
I am standing firm in the Lord - Philippians 4:1
I am living in harmony in the Lord - Philippians 1:2
I am helping others who struggle for the cause of
  Christ - Philippians 4:3
I am rejoicing in the Lord always - Philippians 4:4
I am letting my gentle spirit be known to all - Philippians 4:5
I am not anxious for anything - Philippians 4:6a
I am with thanksgiving praying and letting my requests be
  made known to God - Philippians 4:6b
I am letting the peace of God guard my heart and mind in
  Christ Jesus - Philippians 4:7
I am dwelling on things that are true, honorable, right, pure,
  lovely, of good repute, excellent and all things worthy
  of praise - Philippians 4:8

I am practicing the things I have received, heard
and seen - Philippians 4:9
I am content in whatever circumstances I am in whether
humble or prosperous - Philippians 4:11
I am able to do all things through Christ who strengthens
me - Philippians 4:13
I am sending gifts many times for needs - Philippians 4:16
I AM amply supplies - Philippians 4:18
I am supplied by God with all my needs according to his
riches in glory in Christ Jesus - Philippians 4:19

I am giving thanks to God, the Father of our Lord Jesus Christ
and am praying always for others - Colossians 1:3
I am asking that you may be filled with the knowledge of his
will in all spiritual wisdom and understanding - Colossians 1:9
I am walking in a manner worthy of the Lord, pleasing him
in all respects - Colossians 1:10a
I am bearing fruit in every good work and increasing in
the knowledge of God - Colossians 1:10b
I am strengthened with all power according to his glorious might,
for the attaining of all steadfastness and patience - Colossians 1:11
I am joyously giving thanks to the Father who has qualified us
to share in the inheritance of the saints in light - Colossians 1:12
I am qualified to share in the inheritance of the
saints - Colossians 1:12
I am rescued from the dominion of darkness - Colossians 1:13a
I am transferred to the kingdom of his beloved Son - Colossians 1:13b
I AM created all things - Colossians 1:16a
I AM is the head of the body, the church, he is the beginning
and the first born from the dead - Colossians 1:18
I am reconciled to him so I can be holy, blameless and
irreproachable before him - Colossians 1:22
I am continuing in the faith firmly established and
steadfast - Colossians 1:23
I am rejoicing in my sufferings - Colossians 1:24a
I AM makes known to me the mystery - Colossians 1:27a
I AM, Christ in me, the hope of glory - Colossians 1:27b

I am firmly rooted in Christ - Colossians 2:7a
I am being built up and established in my faith as
  instructed - Colossians 2:7b
I am overflowing with gratitude - Colossians 2:7c
I am proclaiming him, admonishing and teaching every man
  with all wisdom - Colossians 1:28a
I am laboring and striving according to his power which
  mightily works in me - Colossians 1:29
I am attaining to all the wealth that comes from the full assurance
  of understanding, resulting in a true knowledge of God's
  mystery, that is, Christ himself - Colossians 2:2b
I am not deluded by persuasive arguments - Colossians 2:4
I am walking in him, Christ Jesus the Lord - Colossians 2:6
I am firmly rooted in him, being built up in him and
  established in the faith - Colossians 2:7a
I am overflowing with gratitude - Colossians 2:7b
I am not being taken captive through philosophy and
  empty deception or the traditions of men - Colossians 2:8
I am complete in Christ - Colossians 2:10
I am circumcised in him - Colossians 2:11a
I am buried with him in baptism and also raised up with
  him through faith - Colossians 2:12
I am no longer dead in my sins, but alive with
  Christ - Colossians 2:13a
I am alive in him and forgiven of all my sin - Colossians 2:13b
I am hidden with Christ in God - Colossians 3:3
I AM is my life and I will be revealed with him in
  glory - Colossians 3:4
I am chosen of God, holy and beloved - Colossians 3:12a
I am putting on a heart of compassion, kindness, humility,
  gentleness and patience - Colossians 2:12b
I am bearing with and forgiving others as God forgives
  me - Colossians 3:13
I am putting on love, the perfect bond of unity - Colossians 3:14
I am letting the peace of Christ rule in my heart - Colossians 3:15a
I am being thankful - Colossians 3:15b
I am letting the word of Christ richly dwell within

me - Colossians 3:16a

I am with all wisdom teaching and admonishing others with psalms, hymns and spiritual songs, singing with thankfulness in my heart to God - Colossians 3:16b

I am doing all things in the name of the Lord Jesus - Colossians 3:17a

I am giving thanks through Jesus to God the Father - Colossians 3:17b

I am subject to my husband as is fitting in the Lord - Colossians 3:18

I am obedient to my parents in all things - Colossians 3:20

I am doing my work heartily as unto the Lord and not men - Colossians 3:23

I AM is the Lord whom I serve - Colossians 3:24b

I am devoting myself to keeping alert in prayer with an attitude of thanksgiving - Colossians 4:2

I am praying doors will be opened to speak forth the mystery of Christ - Colossians 4:3

I am conducting myself with wisdom toward outsiders and making the most of those opportunities - Colossians 4:5

I am letting my speech always be filled with grace - Colossians 4:6

I am beloved by God and chosen by him - 1 Thessalonians 1:4

I am approved by God and entrusted with the gospel - 1 Thessalonians 2:4

I am walking in a manner worthy of the God who called me into his own kingdom and glory - 1 Thessalonians 2:12

I AM's word performs its work for those who believe - 1 Thessalonians 2:13c

I AM causes his love to abound and increase - 1 Thessalonians 3:12

I am excelling more and more - 1 Thessalonians 4:1c

I AM's will is our sanctification - 1 Thessalonians 4:3

I am making it my ambition to lead a quiet life attending to my own business and work - 1 Thessalonians 4:11

I AM will descend from heaven with a shout... and the dead in Christ will rise up first - 1 Thessalonians 4:16

I AM will meet me in the air and I will always be with him - 1 Thessalonians 4:17

I am a son of the light and day, not of the night or

darkness - 1 Thessalonians 5:5
I am with Jesus whether I am awake or asleep - 1 Thessalonians 5:10
I am encouraging others and building them up - 1 Thessalonians 5:11
I am appreciate those who labor among me - 1 Thessalonians 5:12
I am living in peace with everyone - 1 Thessalonians 5:13
I am admonishing the unruly - 1 Thessalonians 5:14a
I am encouraging the fainthearted - 1 Thessalonians 5:14b
I am helping the weak - 1 Thessalonians 5:14c
I am patient with everyone - 1 Thessalonians 5:14d
I am rejoicing always - 1 Thessalonians 5:16
I am praying without ceasing - 1 Thessalonians 5:17
I am giving thanks in everything - 1 Thessalonians 5:18
I am not quenching the Holy Spirit - 1 Thessalonians 5:19
I am not despising prophetic utterances - 1 Thessalonians 5:20
I am examining everything carefully - 1 Thessalonians 5:21a
I am holding fast to what is good - 1 Thessalonians 5:21b
I am abstaining from every form of evil - 1 Thessalonians 5:22
I AM sanctifies me so my whole spirit, soul and body will
  be blameless at his coming - 1 Thessalonians 5:23
I AM is faithful - 1 Thessalonians 5:24

I am always thanking God for my brothers - 2 Thessalonians 1:3
I am counted worthy of the kingdom of God because of my
  suffering - 2 Thessalonians 1:5
I AM is just - 2 Thessalonians 1:6
I AM gives relief to those who are troubled - 2 Thessalonians 1:7
I AM will overthrow the lawless one with the breath of his
  mouth - 2 Thessalonians 2:8
I AM chose me from the beginning to be saved through the
  sanctifying work of the Spirit - 2 Thessalonians 2:13
I AM is faithful to strengthen and protect me from the evil
  one - 2 Thessalonians 3:3
I am keeping away from every brother who
  is idle - 2 Thessalonians 3:6a
I am never tiring of doing what is right - 2 Thessalonians 3:13

I am dressing modestly and with good deeds - 1 Timothy 2:9

I AM created everything good - 1 Timothy 4:4

I am having nothing to do with godless myths or old wives tales, rather, I am training myself to be godly - 1 Timothy 4:7

I am not neglecting the gift God put inside me - 1 Timothy 4:14

I am helping the widows in my family - 1 Timothy 5:16

I am not sharing in the sins of others and keeping myself pure - 1 Timothy 5:22b

I AM says that godliness with contentment is great gain - 1 Timothy 6:6

I am taking nothing out of this world - 1 Timothy 6:7b

I AM says that the love of money is the root of all kinds of evil - 1 Timothy 6:10a

I am pursuing righteousness, godliness, faith, love, endurance and gentleness - 1 Timothy 6:11

I am fighting the good fight of faith - 1 Timothy 6:12a

I am taking hold of the eternal life to which I was called - 1 Timothy 6:12b

I AM gives life to everything - 1 Timothy 6:13a

I AM is the blessed and only ruler, the King of kings and the Lord of lords - 1 Timothy 6:15

I AM alone is immortal and dwells in unapproachable light - 1 Timothy 6:16

I am putting my hope in God who richly provides everything for our enjoyment - 1 Timothy 6:17

I am rich in good deeds, generous and willing to share - 1 Timothy 6:18

I am guarding what has been entrusted to me - 1 Timothy 6:20

I am turning away from godless chatter that can cause me to wander - 1 Timothy 6:20-21

I am fanning into flame the gift of God - 2 Timothy 1:6

I AM did not give us a spirit of fear - 2 Timothy 1:7

I AM gave me a Spirit of power, love and a sound mind - 2 Timothy 1:7

I am not ashamed to testify about the Lord - 2 Timothy 1:8a

I AM saved me and called me to a holy life for his own purpose and grace - 2 Timothy 1:9

I AM destroyed death and brought life to light through the
   gospel - 2 Timothy 1:10
I am strong in the grace that is in Christ Jesus - 2 Timothy 2:1
I am enduring hardship like a good soldier of Christ
   Jesus - 2 Timothy 2:3
I am not getting involved in civilian affairs - 2 Timothy 2:4
I am doing my best to present myself to God as one approved, not
   ashamed and handling the word of truth correctly - 2 Timothy 2:5
I AM knows those who are his - 2 Timothy 2:19b
I am cleansed and useful to the Master - 2 Timothy 2:21
I am fleeing the evil desires of my youth - 2 Timothy 2:22a
I am calling on the Lord out of a pure heart - 2 Timothy 2:22b
I am not having anything to do with foolish and stupid
   arguments - 2 Timothy 2:23
I am kind to everyone, able to teach and not
   resentful - 2 Timothy 2:24
I AM breathed all scripture, it's useful for teaching, rebuking,
   correcting and for training in righteousness, so that I may be
   thoroughly equipped for every good work - 2 Timothy 3:16-17
I AM will judge the living and the dead - 2 Timothy 4:1
I am preaching the word, in and out of season; correcting,
   rebuking and encouraging with great patience - 2 Timothy 4:2
I am keeping my head in all situations - 2 Timothy 4:5a
I am enduring hardship - 2 Timothy 4:5b
I am doing the work of an evangelist - 2 Timothy 4:5c
I am discharging all the duties of my ministry - 2 Timothy 4:5d
I AM stands at my side and gives me strength - 2 Timothy 4:17a
I AM rescues from the lions mouth - 2 Timothy 4:17c
I am rescued from every evil attack - 2 Timothy 4:18

I AM is he who cannot lie - Titus 1:2
I am above reproach and the husband of one wife, and
   my children believe - Titus 1:6
I am above reproach as God's steward - Titus 1:7a
I am not self willed, or quick tempered, not addicted to
   wine, pugnacious or fond of sordid gain - Titus 1:7b
I am hospitable, loving what is good, sensible, just, devout

and I am self controlled - Titus 1:8
I am holding fast the faithful word - Titus 1:9
I am not a rebellious man, a deceiver or an empty talker - Titus 1:10
I am speaking the things which are fitting for sound
  doctrine - Titus 2:1
I am temperate, dignified, sensible, sound in faith,
  love and perseverance - Titus 2:2
I am reverent in my behavior, not a malicious gossip, enslaved
  to wine and I teach what is good - Titus 2:3
I am encouraging the young women to love their husbands
  and their children - Titus 2:4
I am sensible, pure, kind, work at home and subject to my
  own husband - Titus 2:5
I am an example of good deeds and purity of doctrine - Titus 2:7
I am sound in speech, beyond reproach - Titus 2:8
I am saying no to all ungodliness and worldly passions - Titus 2:12a
I am living a self-controlled, upright and godly life while I
  wait for the blessed hope - Titus 2:12b
I am eager to do what is good - Titus 2:14b
I am subject to rulers and authorities, I am obedient and ready
  for every good deed - Titus 3:1
I am not maligning anyone, I am peaceable, gentle, showing
  every consideration for all men - Titus 3:2
I am saved through the washing of regeneration and renewed
  by the Holy Spirit - Titus 3:5
I am justified by his grace - Titus 3:7a
I am an heir according to the hope of eternal life - Titus 3:7b
I am avoiding foolish controversies, genealogies, strife and
  disputes about the law - Titus 3:9
I am rejecting divisive men - Titus 3:10

I am thanking my God always in prayer for others - Philemon 1:4
I am praying that the fellowship of faith is effective through
  the knowledge of every good thing that is in us for
  Christ's sake - Philemon 1:6
I am having joy and comfort because the hearts of saints
  are being refreshed - Philemon 1:7

I am appealing to others as a prisoner of Christ - Philemon 1:9
I am no longer a slave but a beloved brother - Philemon 1:16

I am paying closer attention to what I hear so that I do not
  drift away from it - Hebrews 2:1
I am made a little lower than the angels - Hebrews 2:7a
I am crowned with glory and honor and appointed over the
  works of his hands - Hebrews 2:7b
I am made perfect through suffering - Hebrews 2:10c
I AM makes men holy - Hebrews 2:11a
I AM is not ashamed to call me his brethren - Hebrews 2:11b
I am tempted in that which I have suffered, to be able to go to
  others who are tempted - Hebrews 2:18
I am a partaker of a heavenly calling - Hebrews 3:1a
I am fixing my thoughts on Jesus, the apostle and high
  priest whom I confess - Hebrews 3:1b
I AM is the builder of everything - Hebrews 3:4
I AM is the faithful son over God's house - Hebrews 3:6a
I am his house as I hold onto the hope which I boast - Hebrews 3:6b
I am hearing his voice and not hardening my heart when
  provoked - Hebrews 3:7
I am encouraging others day after day so that none will be
  hardened by sins deceitfulness - Hebrews 3:13
I am a partaker of Christ and hold fast the beginning of my
  assurance until the end - Hebrews 3:14
I am holding fast my confession that Jesus is the Son of God
  and the great High Priest - Hebrews 4:14
I am drawing near to his throne of grace so I may receive mercy
  and find grace to help in time of need - Hebrews 4:16
I am learning obedience from the things which I suffer - Hebrews 5:8
I am on solid food, training my senses to discern good
  from evil - Hebrews 5:14
I am leaving the elementary teachings about Christ and
  pressing on into maturity - Hebrews 6:1
I am realizing the full assurance of hope - Hebrews 6: 11
I am drawing near to God through a better hop than
  the law - Hebrews 7:19

I am guaranteed a better covenant - Hebrews 7:22
I am cleansed from dead works to serve the living
   God - Hebrews 9:14b
I am cleansed and forgiven by Jesus shed blood - Hebrews 9:22
I am perfected for all time by sanctification - Hebrews 10:14
I am an heir of righteousness according to faith - Hebrews 11:7
I am a stranger and an alien on earth - Hebrews 11:13
I am seeking a country of my own, a better country, a
   heavenly one - Hebrews 11:14-16
I am choosing to endure ill treatment than to enjoy the
   passing pleasures of sin - Hebrews 11:25
I am by faith passing through the Red Sea - Hebrews 11:29
I am by faith conquering kingdom, obtaining promises and
   shutting the mouths of lions - Hebrews 11:33
I am quenching the power of fire, escaping the sword; I am
   made strong and mighty in war - Hebrews 11:34
I am experiencing mocking, scourging, chains and
   imprisonment - Hebrews 11:35
I am surrounded by a great cloud of witnesses - Hebrews 12:1a
I am laying aside every encumbrance and the sin which so
   easily entangles me - Hebrews 12:1b
I am running with endurance the race set before me - Hebrews 12:1c
I am fixing my eyes on Jesus, the author and perfector
   of faith - Hebrews 12:2
I am considering him who endured hostility so I will not
   grow weary or lose heart - Hebrews 12:3
I am disciplined and reproved by God - Hebrews 12:5
I am disciplined and scourged because he (God) loves
   me - Hebrews 12:6
I am disciplined as a son and I endure - Hebrews 12:7
I am disciplined for my own good so that I may share in
   his holiness - Hebrews 12:10
I am trained by discipline and it yields the peaceful fruit
   of righteousness - Hebrews 12:11
I am making strengthening the hands that are weak and the
   knees are feeble - Hebrews 12:12
I am making straight paths for my feet, so that the lame limb

will be healed - Hebrews 12:13

I am pursuing peace with all men and sanctification - Hebrews 12:14

I am seeing to it that no bitter root is springing up to cause trouble - Hebrews 12:15

I am seeing to it that I am not refusing him (Jesus) who is speaking - Hebrews 12:25

I am showing gratitude by which I may offer to God an acceptable service with reverence and awe - Hebrews 12:28

I am not neglecting to show hospitality to strangers - Hebrews 13:2

I am remembering the prisoners and the ill treated - Hebrews 13:3

I am holding marriage in honor - Hebrews 13:4

I am free from the love of money and content with what I have - Hebrews 13:5

I am not afraid for the Lord is my helper, what can man do to me? - Hebrews 13:6

I am imitating the faith of those who have led me - Hebrews 13:7

I am not carried away by strange teachings - Hebrews 13:9

I am sanctified through Jesus own blood - Hebrews 13:12

I am seeking the city which is to come - Hebrews 13:14

I am continually offering up a sacrifice of praise to God and giving thanks to his name - Hebrews 13:15

I am not neglecting to do good and share - Hebrews 13:16

I am obeying my leaders and submitting to them - Hebrews 13:17

I am praying and desiring to conduct myself honorably in all things - Hebrews 13:18

I AM brought up from the dead from the Great Shepherd, Jesus our Lord - Hebrews 13:20

I am equipped in everything to do his good will, to whom be the glory forever and ever. Amen - Hebrews 13:21

I am bearing with the exhortation of this word - Hebrews 13:22

I am a bond servant of the Lord Jesus Christ - James 1:1a

I am considering pure joy when I encounter trials of various kinds - James 1:2

I am letting endurance have its perfect result, so I may be perfect and complete, lacking in nothing - James 1:4

I am asking God for wisdom - James1:5a

I am asking in faith without doubting - James 1:6
I am persevering under trial and once approved I will
  receive the crown of life - James 1:12
I am not being tempted by God - James 1: 13
I am tempted and enticed by my own lust - James 1:14
I am dead when sin is accomplished - James 1:15
I am not deceived - James 1:16
I am given every good and perfect gift from the Father
  of lights above - James 1:17
I AM gives good and perfect gifts – James 1:17a
I AM does not change like shifting shadows – James 1:17b
I am a kind of first fruits among his creatures - James 1:18
I am quick to hear, slow to speak and slow to anger - James 1:19
I am not achieving the righteousness of God
  through anger - James 1:20
I am putting aside all filthiness and the remains of
  wickedness - James 1:21a
I am in humility receiving the implanted word which is able
  to save my soul - James1: 21b
I am a doer of the word and not only a hearer - James 1:22
I am looking intently at the perfect law of liberty and abide
  by it - James 1:25a
I am an effectual doer of the word and I am blessed in
  what I do - James 1:25b
I am bridling my tongue - James 1:26a
I am visiting orphans and widows in their distress - James 1: 27a
I am keeping myself unstained by the world - James 1:27b
I am not making distinctions among us or becoming an
  evil judge - James 2:4
I am chosen to be rich in faith and an heir of the kingdom - James 2:5
I am fulfilling the royal law "love your neighbor as
  yourself" - James 2:8
I am not showing partiality thereby committing sin - James 2:9
I am guilty of all the law even if I only stumble in
  one point - James 2:10
I am speaking and acting as one who will be judged by
  the law of liberty - James 2:12

I am showing mercy which triumphs over judgment - James 2:13
I am showing my faith by my works - James 2:18a
I am the friend of God - James 2:23
I am justified by works and not faith alone - James 2:24
I am with the same mouth blessing God and cursing others,
  this should not be - James 3:9
I am showing the gentleness of wisdom in my good
  behavior - James 3:13
I am submitting to God, resisting the devil and he flees
  from me - James 4:7
I am drawing near to God and he draws near to me - James 4:8a
I am cleansing my hands and purifying my heart - James 4:8b
I am humbling myself before the Lord so he will
  exalt me - James 4:10
I am not speaking against others - James 4:11
I am a vapor that appears for a little while and then
  vanishes away - James 4:14b
I am being patient until the coming of the Lord - James 5:7a
I am strengthening my heart for the coming of the Lord - James 5:8
I am not complaining against the brethren - James 5:9
I am counting those blessed who endure - James5:11
I am letting my yes be yes and my no, no so that I do not
  fall under judgment - James 5:12b
I am praying for those who are suffering - James 5:13a
I am in faith offering prayers for those who are sick and
  the Lord raises them up - James 5:15
I am confessing my sins to another so that I may be
  healed - James 5:16

I am born again to a living hope - 1 Peter 1:3b
I am obtaining an imperishable and undefiled inheritance that
  will not fade away - 1 Peter 1:4
I am protected by the power of God through faith - 1 Peter 1:5
I am preparing my mind for action and I am keeping sober
  in spirit - 1 Peter 1:13
I am not being conformed to my former lusts - 1 Peter 1:14
I am holy in all my behavior - 1 Peter 1:15

I am conducting myself in fear during my stay on earth - 1 Peter 1:17
I am ransomed from the futile ways inherited from my fathers
  by his holy and precious blood - 1 Peter 1:18-19
I am fervently loving others from my heart - 1 Peter 1:22b
I am born again, not of perishable seed, but of
  imperishable seed - 1 Peter 1:23
I am putting aside all malice, deceit, hypocrisy, envy
  and slander - 1 Peter 2:1
I am like a new born baby, long for the pure milk of the word so
  that I may grow up in respect to salvation - 1 Peter 2:2
I am a living stone, being built up as a spiritual house for
  a holy priesthood - 1 Peter 2:5a
I am offering spiritual sacrifices acceptable to God
  through Jesus - 1 Peter 2:5b
I am of a chosen race, a royal priesthood, a holy nation,
  God's own possession - 1 Peter 2:9a
I am proclaiming the excellencies of him who called me
  out of darkness into his marvelous light - 1 Peter 2:9b
I am the people of God and receive mercy - 1 Peter 2:10
I am an alien and a stranger - 1 Peter 2:11a
I am abstaining from fleshly lusts - 1 Peter 2:11b
I am keeping my behavior excellent among the gentiles - 1 Peter 2:12
I am submitting for the Lord's sake to every human
  institution - 1 Peter 2:13
I am acting as a free man, I do not use my freedom as a
  covering for evil, but as a blond slave - 1 Peter 2:16
I am honoring all people, loving the brotherhood, I fear
  God and honor the king - 1 Peter 2:17
I am submissive to my masters, the good and gentle and
  the unreasonable with all respect - 1 Peter 2:18
I am called for this purpose - suffering for Christ as he
  did for me - 1 Peter 2:21
I AM bore my sins in his body on the tree so that I might die
  to sin and live for righteousness and it is by his wounds
  that I have been healed - 1 Peter 2:24
I am submissive to my own husband - 1 Peter 3:1
I am letting my adornment be the hidden person of

the heart - 1 Peter 3:4

I am living with my wife in an understanding way - 1 Peter 3:7

I am in harmony, sympathetic, brotherly, kindhearted and humble in spirit - 1 Peter 3:8

I am not returning evil for evil or insult for insult, rather I give blessing - 1 Peter 3:9a

I am keeping my tongue from evil and my lips from speaking deceit - 1 Peter 3:10b

I am turning away from evil, doing good, seeking peace and pursuing it - 1 Peter 3:11

I am blessed if I suffer for the sake of righteousness - 1 Peter 3:14a

I am not troubled by intimidation - 1 Peter 3:14b

I am setting apart Christ as Lord in my heart - 1 Peter 3:15a

I am prepared to give an answer to everyone who asks for the reason I have hope - 1 Peter 3:15b

I am keeping a clear conscience - 1 Peter 3:16a

I am put to death in the flesh and made alive in the spirit - 1 Peter 3:18b

I am arming myself with the same purpose of Christ - 1 Peter 4:1

I am no longer living in the lust of the flesh - 1 Peter 4:2a

I am living for the will of God - 1 Peter 4:2b

I am no longer doing what the pagans choose to do - 1 Peter 4:3a

I am of sound judgment and sober spirit so that I can pray - 1 Peter 4:7

I am fervent in my love for others, because love covers over a multitude of sins - 1 Peter 4:8

I am hospitable to others without complaint - 1 Peter 4:9

I am using the gifts I've received to serve others faithfully - 1 Peter 4:10a

I am a good steward of the manifold grace of God - 1 Peter 4:10b

I am serving by the strength God provides - 1 Peter 4:11b

I am not surprised at the fiery ordeal among us - 1 Peter 4:12

I am sharing in the sufferings of Christ and I keep on rejoicing - 1 Peter 4:13

I am blessed if I am reviled for the name of Christ - 1 Peter 4:14

I am not ashamed to suffer as a Christian - 1 Peter 4:16

I am entrusting my soul to my faithful Creator by doing

what is right - 1 Peter 4:19
I am proving to be an example to the flock - 1 Peter 5:3
I am clothing myself with humility towards others - 1 Peter 5:5
I am humbling myself under God's mighty hand so he will
  lift me up in due time - 1 Peter 5:6
I am casting all my anxiety on him because he cares
  for me - 1 Peter 5:7
I am self-controlled and alert because my enemy is looking
  to devour me - 1 Peter 5:8
I am resisting him (Satan) and standing firm in the faith - 1 Peter 5:9a
I am restored after suffering a little while - 1 Peter 5:10a
I am perfected, confirmed, strengthened and
  established in him - 1 Peter 5:10b

I am given everything I need for life and godliness through
  my knowledge of Jesus - 2 Peter 1:3
I AM has given us his very great and precious promises, so
  that I may participate in the divine nature and escape the
  corruption of the world caused by evil desires - 2 Peter 1:4
I am making every effort to add to my faith goodness, knowledge,
  self-control, perseverance, godliness, brotherly kindness
  and love. I am possessing these qualities to keep me from
  being ineffective and unproductive in the knowledge
  of Christ - 2 Peter 1:7-8
I am eager to make my calling and election sure so I will never
  fall, so that I may receive a rich welcome into the eternal kingdom
  of our Lord and Savior Jesus Christ - 2 Peter 1:10-11
I am firmly established in the truth - 2 Peter 1:12
I AM did not spare the angels when they sinned - 2 Peter 2:4
I AM did not spare the ancient world, he flooded it - 2 Peter 2:5
I AM condemned the cities of Sodom and Gomorrah - 2 Peter 2:6
I AM rescued Lot - 2 Peter 2:7
I AM knows how to rescue godly men from trials - 2 Peter 2:9
I AM is not slow in keeping his promises - 2 Peter 3:9a
I AM is patient with us - 2 Peter 3:9b
I AM wants no one to perish - 2 Peter 3:9c
I AM wants everyone to come to repentance - 2 Peter 3:9d

I am looking forward to the day of God coming - 2 Peter 3:12
I am looking forward to the new heavens and the new earth,
  the home of righteousness - 2 Peter 3:13
I am making every effort to be found spotless, blameless and
  at peace with God - 2 Peter 3:14b
I am on guard so I will not be carried away by the error of
  lawless men and fall from my secure position - 2 Peter 3:17
I am growing in the grace and knowledge of my Lord and Savior,
  Jesus Christ, to him be the glory - 2 Peter 3:18

I am forgiven, cleansed from all unrighteousness - 1 John 1:9
I AM has forgiven our sins for his names sake - 1 John 2:12
I am not loving the world or the things in it - 1 John 2:15
I am anointed by the holy one - 1 John 2:20
I am promised eternal life - 1 John 2:25
I AM anoints me and abides in me - 1 John 2:27a
I AM's anointing teaches me all things - 1 John 2:27b
I am abiding and having confidence in him - 1 John 2:28
I AM is righteous - 1 John 2:29
I AM's love for me is great! - 1 John 3:1
I am called a child of God and he loves me -1 John 3:1
I am purified as I fix my hope on him - 1 John 3:3
I AM appeared to take away sins – 1 John 3:5
I AM, the Son of God appeared to destroy the works of
  the devil - 1 John 3:8
I am not practicing sin because I have been born of God - 1 John 3:9
I am loving others - 1 John 3:11
I am laying down my life for the brethren - 1 John 3:16
I am not loving with word or tongue but in deed
  and truth - 1 John 3:18
I am confident before God that whatever I ask of him, I receive
  because my heart does not condemn me, for I keep his commands
  and do those things that are pleasing unto him - 1 John 3:21-22
I am believing in the name of his son, Jesus Christ - 1 John 3:23a
I am obeying his commands, I live in him and he in me - 1 John 3:24a
I am testing the spirits to see if they are from God - 1 John 4:1
I am of God and have overcome them - 1 John 4:4a

I am of God and he who is in me is greater than he who
is in the world - 1 John 4:4b
I am from God, therefore I know the spirit of truth and the
spirit of error - 1 John 4:6
I AM is the propitiation for our sins - 1 John 4:10b
I am abiding in him and he in me because he has given me
his spirit - 1 John 4:13
I am confessing that Jesus is the Son of God, God abides in
him and he in God - 1 John 4:15
I AM perfects me in love that I may not fear - 1 John 4:18
I am believing that Jesus is the Christ born of God - 1 John 5:1
I am keeping his commandments and they are not
burdensome - 1 John 5:3
I am overcoming the world by my faith - 1 John 5:3
I am confident that he hears me when I ask according to
his will - 1 John 5:14
I am born of God and the evil one cannot touch me - 1 John 5:18
I am in him who is true - 1 John 5:20b
I am guarding myself from idols - 1 John 5:21

I am walking according to his commandments and
this is love - 2 John 1:6
I am watching myself so that I may receive a full reward - 2 John 1:8

I am prospering in all respects, I am in good health - 3 John 1:2
I am walking in truth - 3 John 1:3
I am joyful when I hear that my children are walking in
the truth - 3 John 1:4
I am acting faithfully in whatever I accomplish for the brethren
that are strangers - 3 John 1:5
I am a fellow worker as I support the brethren - 3 John 1:8
I am not imitating what is evil but what is good - 3 John 1:11

I am called and beloved by God the father and I am kept for
Jesus Christ - Jude 1:1
I am contending earnestly for the faith - Jude 1:3b
I am building myself up in the most holy faith - Jude 1:20a

I am praying in the spirit - Jude 1:20b
I am keeping myself in the love of God - Jude 1:21
I AM is able to keep me from stumbling and he makes me to stand
in the presence of his glory, blameless and with great joy - Jude 1:24

I AM communicates through his angels - Revelation 1:1
I am blessed to read, hear and heed the words of the
prophecy - Revelation 1:3
I AM is, was and is to come - Revelation 1:4b
I AM is the Faithful Witness, the first born from the dead
and the ruler of all the kings of the earth - Revelation 1:5a
I AM loves us and has released us from our sins - Revelation 1:5b
I AM made us to be a kingdom and priests to God
the Father - Revelation 1:6a
I AM is coming on the clouds - Revelation 1:7
I AM is the Alpha and Omega, the Almighty One - Revelation 1:8
I AM is the First and the Last - Revelation 1:17b
I AM is the living one, alive forevermore - Revelation 1:18a
I AM has the keys of death and hades - Revelation 1:18b
I AM holds the seven stars in his right hand and walks among
the seven golden lampstands - Revelation 2:1
I AM will grant those who overcome to eat of the tree of life
in the paradise of God - Revelation 2:7b
I AM is the first and last who was dead and has come to life
I AM has the sharp two edged sword - Revelation 2:8b
I AM will give to those who overcome some of the
hidden manna - Revelation 2:17b
I AM will give to those who overcome a white stone with a
new name written on it - Revelation 2:17c
I AM is the Son of God - Revelation 2:18b
I AM is he who searches minds and hearts and gives us
according to our deeds - Revelation 2:23b
I AM will cloth us who overcome in white garments and confess
our names before the Father and his angels - Revelation 3:5
I AM is holy and true - Revelation 3:7b
I AM has the key of David, who opens and no one shuts and
who shuts and no one opens - Revelation 3:7c

I AM is, the Amen - Revelation 3:14b
I AM is the Faithful and True Witness - Revelation 3:14c
I AM is the beginning of the creation of God - Revelation 3:14d
I AM reproves those he loves - Revelation 3:19
I AM stands at the door and knocks - Revelation 3:20
I AM overcame and sat down with his Father - Revelation 3:21b
I AM is worthy to receive glory, honor and power - Revelation
I AM is the Lion of the tribe of Judah, the root
  of David - Revelation 5:5b
I AM made us to be a kingdom and a priest to him - Revelation 5:10
I am a priest to God - Revelation 5:10
I AM is the LAMB who is worthy to be slain - Revelation 5:12
I AM will reign forever and ever - Revelation 11:15b
I am an over-comer by the blood of the Lamb - Revelation 12:11a
I AM is the King of the ages - Revelation 15:3
I AM, the Lamb, he is the Lord of lords and the King
  of kings - Revelation 17:14
I AM , the LORD our God, the Almighty reigns - Revelation 19:6
I AM is Faithful and True and in righteousness he judges and
  wages war - Revelation 19:11b
I AM is the Word of God - Revelation 19:13c
I AM rules with an iron scepter - Revelation 19:15b
I AM is the Alpha and the Omega, the Beginning and
  the End - Revelation 21:6b
I AM gives to the thirsty water from the spring of life
  without cost - Revelation 21:6c
I am the wife of the Lamb - Revelation 21:9
I AM the Lamb are its temple - Revelation 21:22
I AM has illumined the city, its lamp is the Lamb - Revelation 21:23
I AM is coming quickly - Revelation 22:7
I AM is the Alpha and Omega, the Fist and the Last the
  Beginning and the End - Revelation 22:13
I AM is the root and descendant of David - Revelation 22:16b
I AM is the Bright and Morning Star - Revelation 22:16c
I am taking of the water of life without cost - Revelation 22:17c

I AM is Coming Again!

Hallelujah!
Thank you Jesus!

They overcame him by the blood of the Lamb and the word of their testimony. Revelation 12:11a ~ This is one of my favorite scriptures, ohh, the blood of Jesus and the word of our testimony~ it's not only God's power to deliver us, it's his power to set us free that frees us to be overcomers in every single way! I am including these additional documents so that you can have an idea of how the Holy Spirit has guided me, in and through my trials. I pray that you too will begin declaring the emphatic truth of God's word for yourself! Whom the Son has set free~ is free indeed!

Let me ask you, has the Son set you free so that without a doubt you can say: I consider it pure joy whenever I face trials of many kinds because I know it's for the strengthening of my faith? I pray it is!

Although God's word is free, it comes with a high price. May I encourage you to draw upon the Holy Spirits guidance as have I and many others as well. As you read through this section I pray you will discover for yourself just who your Heavenly Father is and what his great and glorious promises for you are. You are a child of the Most High God and the time you invest in his word will determine your return. Based on the following scriptures, when you seek (and keep on seeking) you shall surely find! Why? Because that's his promise and we know that all of his promises are ~ Yes and Amen!

Ask and it will be given to you, seek and you will find, knock and the door will be opened to you. For everyone who asks receives, the one who seeks finds and to the one who knocks, the door will be opened. Matthew 7:7-8

You will seek me and find me when you seek me with all your heart. Jeremiah 29:13

As you continue in his word and discover these truths for yourself, begin confessing them so that you will, with all the saints, be appropriating the richest of all inheritances from our Father above, for he it is, who loves you! My prayer is that you will be led to create your own confessions of faith and that his word would become like a delicacy that you would never cease to crave. Amen and Amen!

Please note that what follows is not in any particular order so feel free to review them in any order you feel led to. You will see that the scripture verses themselves are in bold print and the personalization's are in regular type with the words of Jesus being bold and italicized. As you proceed I trust you will be mightily encouraged with and through the word!

You desire but do not have, so you kill. You covet but you cannot get what you want, so you quarrel and fight. You do not have because you do not ask God. When you ask, you do not receive, because you ask with wrong motives, that you may spend what you get on your pleasures. James 4:2-3

According to this verse, we have not because we ask not. So lets not just be seekers and knockers let's be askers as well. Amen and Amen!

In this section I have included documents we used in the Healing School as well as my personal declarations. You will see that some of the documents were created based upon others writings which are duly noted on each of them.

I have learned that because the word of God is free, the only copyright in this work is that if you want to copy something, copy it right away and give credit where credit is due!

One last note~ if you find any typos or incorrect scripture references, please correct them for yourself and then please forgive me. Thank you and the Lord bless you!

May you be blessed as you continue to hide God's word in your heart so that you may "know him more and more and more and more"!

Faith Talk – Positive Confessions of Faith

Speak this daily so that your mind is transformed.
Continue speaking it until your faith is built up so that you
will keep your healing despite continuing attacks.

Surely he took up our infirmities and carried our sorrows. Isaiah 53:4a **Surely he took up our infirmities and carried our diseases.** Matthew 8:17 ~ Since God took my sicknesses and pains, surely I don't need to carry them. Jesus took them along with my sins and bore them for me on the cross.

He himself bore our sins in his body on the tree, so that we might die to sins and live for righteousness; by his wounds, you have been healed. 1 Peter 2:24 ~ Now I live for righteousness and I am dead to sins. Not I *will* be healed or I *might* be healed~ but, *I was healed when Christ was on the cross.*

God's word is just as true when Satan tries to put sickness on me as when I feel great. **I walk by faith, not by sight.** 2 Corinthians 5:7 ~ I walk not only by faith, but in hope! I pay no attention to the symptoms my eyes see or my body feels. I choose to believe God and his word. I am healed in Jesus' name.

Praise be to the God and Father of our Lord Jesus Christ, who has blessed us in the heavenly realms with every spiritual blessing in Christ. Ephesians 1:3 ~ God's already done it, he *has* given us the blessings. God has already healed me and provided for me, because this is what his word declares and so do I. (period)

The Lord is my Shepherd, I shall not be in want. Psalm 23:1 ~ I believe the Lord, *he is my Shepherd and I shall not be in want*!

My God shall supply all your need according to his riches in glory in Christ Jesus. Philippians 4:19 ~ I have everything I need. Satan, I don't believe your lies. If I really needed it, the word says I have it and God supplies it! And I don't just have *it*, but I have *all* of it. It isn't "just barely enough" it is "according to his riches in glory". Thank you Jesus, your supply is enough for me.

I answer how I feel according to the word, not my physical senses for I walk by faith and not by sight. I say, "according to God's word, I am healed!" I don't say "I will be healed or I might be healed," I say "I am healed!"

Satan brings doubt and confusion into my mind and that's where I fight the battles. **We take captive every thought to make it obedient to Christ.** 2 Corinthians 10:5b ~ I will always win the battles by turning my thoughts to Christ.

I stand on the word and believe I receive. I am ready in the word, having read it, prayed it and meditated on it, I stand firm and I don't waver. **I have been crucified with Christ and I no longer live, but**

Christ lives in me. The life I live in the body, I live by faith in the Son of God, who loved me and gave himself for me. Galatians 2:20

Confession is testifying to something I know. I line up my confession of faith with what the Bible says. 1 John 4:4b says: **The one who is in you is greater than the one who is in the world.**

Therefore, there is now no condemnation for those who are in Christ Jesus. Romans 8:1 ~ I am in Christ Jesus right now, no condemnation can stand against me.

I believe that those things which I say and do not doubt will come to pass and I shall have what I say. *Therefore I tell you, whatever you ask for in prayer, believe that you have received it, and it will be yours.* Mark 11:24 ~ I believe that I have faith, blessings, health, provision for my needs, wisdom and spiritual gifts. I have everything I need. I am content, resting in God's promises. **For no matter how many promises God has made, they are "Yes" in Christ.** 2 Corinthians 1:20a

I confess what is mine according to God's word. **No, in all these things we are more than conquerors through him who loved us.** Romans 8:37 ~ There is no failure for me when I am in Christ Jesus. **Therefore, if anyone is in Christ, he is a new creation; the old has gone, the new has come!** 2 Corinthians 5:17 ~ I am a new creation.

Do you not know that your body is a temple of the Holy Spirit, who is in you, whom you have received from God? 1 Corinthians 6:19 ~ My body is a temple of the Holy Spirit, there is no room for anything that is not holy or of God in it. I refuse to give place to illness or disease.

In Deuteronomy 28:16-44 the curse of the law is explained in detail, including every sickness and disease, poverty, defeat by your enemies and death. But praise God ~ I am redeemed from the curse of the law. **Christ redeemed us from the curse of the law by becoming a curse for us.** Galatians 3:13a ~ **For this reason Christ is the mediator of a new covenant, that those who are called may receive the promised eternal inheritance– now that he has died as a ransom to set them free from the sins committed under the first covenant.** Hebrews 9:15 ~ I have a new and better covenant. **He sets aside the first to establish the second.** Hebrews 10:9b

In him we have redemption through his blood. Ephesians 1:7a ~ I'm not going to have it, not trying to have it, but I have it *now*! **For in him we live and move and have our being.** Acts 17:28a ~ My very life is in him.

For he has rescued us from the dominion of darkness and brought us into the kingdom of the Son he loves. Colossians 1:13 ~ I have been delivered from the power of darkness into the very kingdom of

God. **If God is for us, who can be against us?** Romans 8:31b

For God did not give us a spirit of timidity, but a spirit of power, of love and of self discipline. 2 Timothy 1:7 (KJV) ~ I have the spirit of power, love and self discipline in me, because that's what God has given me!

Resist the devil, and he will flee from you. James 4:7b ~ I resist the devil and he does flee from me.

So do not fear for I am with you, do not be dismayed, for I am your God. I will strengthen you and help you, I will uphold you with my righteous right hand. Isaiah 41:10

Cast all your anxiety on him because he cares for you.
1 Peter 5:7 ~ I cast all my cares on him, knowing he cares for me.

God is our refuge and strength, an ever-present help in trouble.
Psalm 46:1 ~ God is my refuge and my helper.

I, even I, am he who blots out your transgressions for my own sake, and remembers your sins no more. Isaiah 43:25 ~ Hallelujah, *I AM* blots out my transgressions and he forgets, he forgets my sin!

I have seen his ways, but I will heal him. I will guide him and

restore comfort to him, creating praise on the lips of the mourners in Israel. Peace, peace, to those far and near, says the LORD. "And I will heal them." Isaiah 57:18-19 ~ Even though God has seen my ways, (he sees it all ya know), he will heal me.

I will never leave you nor forsake you. Joshua 1:5b ~ He is my helper who will never leave of forsake me!

God's word is true regardless of my feelings or my circumstances. **Forever, O Lord, thy word is settled in heaven.** Psalm 119:89

My faith is not in what my senses see or hear. My faith is in God. **The God who gives life to the dead and calls things that are not as though they were.** Romans 4:17b ~ I am strong in faith, giving glory to God. I am fully persuaded that what God has promised, he is able to deliver. I don't consider my own body but I think on God in his glory, the author and finisher of my faith and on Jesus, the high priest who took my infirmities and bore my illnesses. I am fixing my eyes on Jesus and calling into being those things that are yet not!

I do not consider and see the wrong thing. I consider who God is and what his book says. I don't deny pain, I simply acknowledge that Satan sends it, then I continue to think on Jesus, my intercessor and high priest. I think on what he's done and is doing for me, I praise and thank him, holding fast to my confession of faith. Jesus died for me, not for himself. He bore my sin, not his own. He bore my sicknesses and diseases, not his own, he died and rose for me. He ascended into heaven to speak for me. He's up there now saying what he did for me, so Satan, leave me. I submit to the Lord, resist you and watch you flee in Jesus name.

Jesus did it for me on the cross and he will do it in me. He redeemed me and when I abide in him I have full redemption of life, health, strength, soundness, comfort, purity, holiness, peace and joy. The old things (disease, weakness, doubt, lack, pain, sorrow, depression, sadness) are passed away for I am a new creature in Christ. I take hold of God's strength to live a holy pleasing life unto him.

"My grace is sufficient for you, for my power is made perfect in weakness." 2 Corinthians 12:9a ~ **That's why for Christ's sake, I delight in weaknesses, in insults, in hardships, in persecutions and in difficulties. For when I am weak then I am strong.** 2 Corinthians 12:10 ~ Notice Paul does not say in sickness, pain or disease. Here he names afflictions that come against Christians.

God's strength is made perfect in my weakness. I gladly forsake all of myself in exchange for all of Christ. **And my God will meet all your needs.** Philippians 4:19a ~ This applies not only to the need for healing but to the need for strength as well. While I may be weak or sick in my body, I choose to honor and glorify God with it as I am made in his image, in his strength. **Let the weak say, I *am* strong!** Joel 3:10b So then, I too can say I am strong, not I shall be strong, but I am strong! This verse says that it isn't the strong who say, but the weak who say. Please also note that the verse says to "say" we are~ not just to "think" it. So let's say it out loud~ I am strong in the mighty strength of the Lord!

I do what seems impossible in the strength God gives me. **"But those who hope in the LORD shall renew *their* strength.** Isaiah 40:31a ~ I can do all things through Christ! **I can do <u>all</u> things through Christ who strengthens me.** Philippians 4:13 It does say, all things right!

God works in me with the same mighty power he worked in Jesus when I believe him. **I pray also that the eyes of your heart may be enlightened in order that you may know the hope to which he has called you, the riches of his glorious inheritance in the saints, and his incomparably great power for us who believe. That power is like the working of his mighty strength which he exerted in Christ when he raised him from the dead.** Ephesians 1:18-20a

I overcome Satan by the blood of the Lamb and the word of my testimony. I hold fast believing God's remedy always accomplishes what he says. The name of Jesus *always* overcomes Satan. **They overcame him** (Satan) **by the blood of the Lamb and by the word of their testimony.** Revelation 12:11a

I watch vigilantly for Satan never stops looking for opportunities to devour us. I overcome Satan, rousing myself to greater intensity in the things of God. Never in this life do I get to a place where Satan cannot attack me, but God is not willing that I be overcome even once. **Be self-controlled and alert. Your enemy the devil prowls around like a roaring lion looking for someone to devour. Resist him, standing firm in the faith.** 1 Peter 5:8-9a ~ **The Lord will rescue me from every evil attack.** 2 Timothy 4:18a

I will praise God in faith, even before I receive the blessings from him. **Be joyful always.** 1Thessalonians 5:16 ~ I rejoice at all times for this is the will of God. **Give thanks in all circumstances, for this is God's will for you in Christ Jesus.** 1Thessalonians 5:18 ~ I am thankful in all things, even when I am despised, rejected or see no way out, if I am without friends or when my labor appears wasted, I will give thanks.

The joy of the LORD is your strength. Nehemiah 8:10b ~ As I rejoice and praise him, God replaces sorrow with joy. My joy attracts others to God. God meets me when I rejoice. I rejoice in Christ and not in "things or circumstances." **Though the fig tree does not bud and there are no grapes on the vines, though the olive crop fails, and the fields produce no food, though there are no sheep in the pen and no cattle in the stalls, yet I will rejoice in the Lord, I will be joyful in God my Savior.** Habakkuk 3:17-18

Pray continually. 1Thessalonians 5:17 ~ I pray without ceasing. I ask, "Lord, how can I please you? How shall I do this to bring honor and glory to your name? Enable me to honor you." I talk to God unceasingly in every step I take. Proverbs 3:6 says: **In all your ways acknowledge him and he will make your paths straight.** I acknowledge God in all my ways and he makes my paths straight.

I thank him in everything ~ in blessings, answered prayer, for his presence, joy, peace, strength, healings AND in disappointments, hardships, privations, sufferings, lessons, losses, crosses, attacks of the enemy, desertions, neglects and misrepresentations, as these are the instruments God uses to conform me to the exact image of his son.

When I receive them with thanksgiving instead of begging God to take them away, I overcome in Jesus' name with a thankful heart and reign in life. *Why does the list not include sickness or disease, because Jesus gives us authority over that kind of attack.* **For if, by the trespass of the one man, death reigned through that one man, how much more will those who receive God's abundant provision of grace and of the gift of righteousness reign in life through the one man Jesus Christ.** Romans 5:17

When I do my best for God and walk in his word, when people find fault, criticize, judge or condemn, I endure quietly. **Endure hardship**

with us like a good soldier of Christ Jesus. 2 Timothy 2:3 ~ I remain sweet, gentle, meek and lowly with never a word against them, never a look or a feeling. I bear with longsuffering and joyfulness that I am counted worthy to suffer for Christ. I work on, as Paul did that I may endure. In due season, I trust I shall reap. **And the God of all grace, who called you to his eternal glory in Christ, after you have suffered a little while, will himself restore you and make you strong, firm and steadfast.** 1 Peter 5:10

I do not murmur, talk nor change my purpose. I endure to the end, persevering in all things, in joy and thanksgiving. Jesus Christ and the Holy Spirit are always interceding for me and I am made nigh (close) by his blood. How blessed I am to be drawn near to God in these days. The blood gives me access to his face where I discover his love and willingness to give what he has promised. I ask God in boldness for favor with people and access to their hearts, it's not through self effort, but through the blood that we are made perfect to God in every good work.

Hebrews 10:19 says his blood gives us access to the Holy of Holies where we are shut away from evil to praise and worship our Lord. The blood shuts out the clamor of voices that keeps us away from God. Satan has no claim on me for I am covered by the power of the blood of Jesus. Worship wins the war, Hallelujah!

Ephesians 2:16 and Colossians 1:20 say that all things are reconciled by the power of the blood. Whenever and in whatever way the enemy comes, he is shut out and we overcome by the blood of the Lamb and the word of our testimony!

I am not surprised when my faith undergoes trials. **Dear friends, do not to be surprised at the painful trial you are suffering, as though something strange were happening to you.** 1 Peter 4:12 ~ Often the trial may be that symptoms remain for a while, but 1 John 4:4b says: **Greater is he that is in you than he that is in the world.**

My own mouth gives testimony to what I believe and hastens the victory. I say that anger, unforgiveness, worry, confusion, pain, disease, doubt or evil will have no place in me. I will not have them. I refuse to accept them, recognize them or own them, I am delivered regardless of how it looks or feels. I praise God for what he's done already on the cross.

Let us not become weary in doing good, for at the proper time we will reap a harvest if we do not give up. Galatians 6:9 ~ I stir myself up to put away doubt, confusion, half-heartedness, luke-warmness, waverings and unbelief. I take hold of God's heart, his word and his promises that will sustain me so that I may reap the harvest.

Hold on to what you have. Revelation 3:11b ~ Satan tries to take it away by bringing in doubt and getting us to take our eyes off Jesus and see only the wind as Peter did, but we rebuke him and stand firm. Then Jesus said, *"Did I not tell you that if you believed, you would see the glory of God?"* John 11:40 ~ I believe, do you? Genesis 28:15 says: **"I will not leave you until I have done that which I have promised you."**

I do not "feel" my faith, I act on it. God confirms our faith with signs when we act on what we really believe. **And the Lord worked with them and confirmed his word by the signs that accompanied it.** Mark 16:20b

I have the authority over Satan, delegated to me from Jesus. I have been seated with Christ high above the principalities and powers of Satan. My feelings and fears do not negate the power and authority God gave me through Christ Jesus. I have already been delivered into the kingdom of God's dear Son, giving me the right and authority and the delegated power to banish Satan according to Colossians 1:13, 3:1 and Ephesians 1:21

They will place their hands on sick people, and they will get well. Mark 16:18c ~ When I lay my hands on sick people, I exercise my authority over Satan and they will recover. According to the word, that authority is mine whether I feel like I've got it or not. Whether or not I exercise my authority is also up to me. I must *choose* to exercise authority over my enemies in Jesus' name.

And do not give the devil a foothold. Ephesians 4:27 ~ Satan cannot take a place we don't give him. Satan is running the world system but we are not of the world. God has through Christ reconciled us to himself, he brought us from hatred to friendship. I am reconciled to him, not he to me.

I defeat Satan because I have a foundation in God's word. I act on it in faith by the Holy Spirit while remaining steadfast thanking God for Christ's victory. I wait patiently and expectantly, for what God has promised *is* already done. God's ways are not the world's ways. His ways are higher, exceedingly beyond anything I can hope or imagine.

Many are the afflictions of the righteous, but the LORD delivers him out of them all. Psalm 34:19

Faith brings the unseen into being and makes the unfelt things real to the senses. It pleases God when I look only at his word. It pleases him when I base my faith on his promise. Faith sees sickness as part of the curse of the Law. Faith sees the power of sickness as abolished at Calvary. Faith commands in Jesus' name and stands in quiet assurance that what the Bible says, will come to pass.

When symptoms of sickness may linger, faith declares it is done because God's word says so. Satan is a liar and says God never did it and that he never will do it. Although Satan is the father of lies, Jesus came to bring not only life, he came to give us an abundant life.

For those of us who believe and choose to trust in him, our job is to step into it, that is faith ~ through declaring the truth of his word.

When doubts come, they must be cast off and the word of God repeated (often many times) to keep standing in faith. We must leave the results, the timing and the methods to God knowing that according to his word~ it shall come to pass.

The confessions above are based partly on the writings of:
Ken Hagin and Mrs. C. Nuzum.

Greater Works Ministries 2006

Faith and Authority

I praise you Lord for Jesus' example of using the Bible, your word, to fight Satan. I am and will do the same as Jesus, my Lord, as I repeat these words of faith from your word, the Bible.

Isaiah 53:4-5 **Surely he took up our infirmities and carried our sorrows, yet we considered him stricken by God, smitten by him, and afflicted. But he was pierced for our transgressions, he was crushed for our iniquities; the punishment that brought us peace was upon him, and by his wounds we are healed.** Since God took my sicknesses and pains, surely I don't need to carry them. Jesus took them along with my sins and bore them for me on the cross.

1 Peter 2:24 **He himself bore our sins in his body on the tree, so that we might die to sins and live for righteousness, it's by his wounds, you have been healed.** Now I live for righteousness and I am dead to sins. Not I will be healed or I might be healed, but, I was already healed when Christ was on the cross.

2 Corinthians 5:7 **We live by faith, not by sight.** God's word is just as true when Satan tries to put sickness on me as when I feel great. I walk not only by faith, but in hope! I pay no attention to the symptoms my eyes see or my body feels. I choose to believe God and his word. I am healed in Jesus' name. I answer how I feel according

to the word, not my physical senses for I walk by faith and so I say, "according to God's word, *I am healed!*"

Ephesians 1:3 **Praise be to the God and Father of our Lord Jesus Christ, who has blessed us in the heavenly realms with every spiritual blessing in Christ.** You are holy and awesome Lord, thank you that you have already blessed me with every spiritual blessing in heavenly places in Christ Jesus. I am not awaiting blessing I am walking in blessing right now.

Philippians 4:19 **My God shall supply all your need according to his riches in glory in Christ Jesus.** Psalm 23:1 **The Lord is my Shepherd, I shall not be in want.** I have everything I need. Satan, I don't believe your lies. If I really needed it, the word says I have it and God supplies it! I don't just have a bit of it, I have all of it, it's according to his riches in glory. Thank-you Jesus!

2 Corinthians 10:5 **We demolish arguments and every pretension that sets itself up against the knowledge of God, and we take captive every thought to make it obedient to Christ.** Satan brings doubt and confusion into my mind and thoughts which is where I fight the battles. I win the battles by turning my thoughts to Jesus.

Galatians 2:20 **I have been crucified with Christ and I no longer live, but Christ lives in me. The life I live in the body, I live by**

faith in the Son of God, who loved me and gave himself for me. I stand on the word and believe I receive. I am ready in the word, having read it, prayed it and meditated on it. Acts 17:28a **For in him we live and move and have our being.**

Romans 8:1 **Therefore, there is now no condemnation for those who are in Christ Jesus.** No condemnation can stand against me for I am in Christ Jesus right now.

Mark 11:24 *Therefore I tell you, whatever you ask for in prayer, believe that you have received it, and it will be yours.* I believe that those things which I say and do not doubt will come to pass and that I shall have what I say. I believe that I have faith, blessings, health, provision, wisdom and spiritual gifts. I have everything I need. I am content, resting in God's promises. 2 Corinthians 1:20a **For no matter how many promises God has made, they are "Yes" and "Amen" in Christ.**

Romans 8:37 **No, in all these things we are more than conquerors through him who loved us.** I confess what is mine according to God's word. There is no failure for me when I am in Christ Jesus.

1 Corinthians 6:19 **Do you not know that your body is a temple of the Holy Spirit who is in you, whom you have received from God?** My body is a temple of the Holy Spirit, there is no room for anything

that is not holy or that which is not of God in it. I refuse to give any place to illness, sickness, disease or death.

Galatians 3:13a **Christ redeemed us from the curse of the law by becoming a curse for us.** The curse of the law is explained in detail in Deuteronomy, including every sickness and disease, poverty, defeat and death. But praise God! I am redeemed from the curse of the law, I have a new and better covenant.

Hebrews 9:15 **For this reason Christ is the mediator of a new covenant, that those who are called may receive the promised eternal inheritance- now that he has died as a ransom to set them free from the sins committed under the first covenant.** Hebrews 10:9b **He sets aside the first to establish the second.**

Ephesians 1:7a **In him we have redemption through his blood.** I'm not going to have it, not trying to have it, I have it now!

2 Timothy 1:7-8a **For God did not give us a spirit of timidity, but a spirit of power, of love and of self -discipline.** So do not be ashamed to testify about our Lord. I have the spirit of power, love and self-discipline in me and I have the mind of Christ that I may boldly proclaim Christ without shame.

Romans 4:17b **The God who gives life to the dead and calls things**

that are not as though they were. My faith is not in what my senses see and hear, my faith is in God. I am strong in faith giving glory to God. I am fully persuaded that what God has promised he is able to deliver. I do not consider my own body but I think on God in his glory. I fix my eyes on Jesus the author and finisher of my faith, the high priest who took my infirmities and bore my illnesses. I do not consider and see the wrong thing, I consider who God is and what his word says. I do not deny pain, I just acknowledge that Satan sends it, then I continue to think on Jesus, my intercessor and high priest. I think on what he's done and is doing for me and I praise and thank him, holding fast to my confession of faith. Jesus died for me, he bore my sin, sicknesses and diseases, not his own, he died and arose for me. He ascended into heaven, so Satan, leave me~ I resist you in Jesus name. Jesus did it on the cross~ he redeemed me so I have full redemption of life, health, strength, soundness, comfort, purity, holiness, peace and joy. The old things (disease, doubt, lack, pain, weakness, sorrow, depression and sadness) are passed away, for I am a new creature in Christ. I take hold of God's strength to live a holy life pleasing to him.

My own mouth gives testimony to what I believe and hastens the victory. I say that anger, worry, pain, unforgiveness, confusion, disease, doubt or evilness have no place in me. I will not have them. I refuse to accept them, recognize them or own them, I am delivered regardless of how it looks or feels. I praise God for what he's done already on the cross. I stir myself up as I put away half-heartedness, luke-warmness, doubt, confusion, waverings and unbelief and I take hold of God's heart, his word and his promises. Satan tries to take it away by bringing in doubt and getting me to take my eyes off Jesus and see only the wind as Peter did, but I rebuke him and stand firm. I have the authority over Satan delegated to me from Jesus. I have been seated with Christ high above the principalities and powers. My feelings and fears do not negate the power and authority God gave me through Jesus. I have already been delivered into the kingdom of God's dear Son giving me the right and authority and the delegated power to banish Satan.

Mark 16:17-18 *And these signs will accompany those who believe~ In my name they will drive out demons; they will speak in new tongues; they will pick up snakes with their hands; and when they drink deadly poison, it will not hurt them at all; they will place their hands on sick people, and they will get well.* I am a believer! These signs accompany my belief: I drive out demons, I speak in new tongues, I pick up snakes with my hands and when I drink deadly poison, I am not hurt at all. When I lay my hands on sick people they do get well. Thank-you Jesus! And according to the word that authority is mine whether I feel like I've got it or not, I <u>choose</u> to exercise my authority over Satan in Jesus' name. Faith brings the unseen into being and makes the unfelt things real to the senses. It pleases God when I look only at his word and when I base my faith on his promises. Faith sees sickness as part of the curse of the Law; faith also sees the power of sickness as abolished at Calvary. Faith commands in Jesus' name and stands in quiet assurance that what the Bible says will come to pass. When symptoms of sickness linger, faith declares it is done because God's word says so. Jesus came to bring abundant life so when doubts come, I cast them off with the word of God as I stand in faith. I leave the results, the timing and the methods to God, knowing that according to his word, it shall come to pass.

The confessions above are based partly on the writings of Ken Hagin and C. Nuzum.

Matthew 28:18 **Then Jesus came to them and said, *"All authority in heaven and on earth has been given to me."*** Jehovah God, I praise you that all authority, power and dominion in heaven and earth have been given to Jesus. He is the perfect keeper of all.

2 Timothy 4:17-18 **But the Lord stood at my side and gave me strength, so that through me the message might be fully proclaimed and all the Gentiles might hear it. And I was delivered from the lion's mouth. The Lord will rescue me from every evil attack and will bring me safely to his heavenly kingdom. To him be glory forever and ever. Amen!** Yes, the Lord gives me strength, I fully proclaim his good news so everyone can hear. He delivers me from Satan's attempts to devour me and he rescues me from every evil attack. Hallelujah!

John 10:10 **The thief comes only to steal and kill and destroy, I have come that they may have life and have it to the full.** What a contrast! Satan, you come to steal, kill and destroy me, but my Lord and Savior Jesus Christ came that I would have life and have it abundantly! I believe him and not you. I see your deception and destruction and theft for what it is.

Ephesians 6:10 **Finally, be strong in the Lord and in his mighty power.** God's word says to be strong in the Lord and in the power of his might. If God says to be strong in the power of his might, it is possible to do so. I thank you God that I am strong in the power of your might. Jesus gave me power and authority when he defeated Satan through his death and resurrection. That power belongs to me as part of the body of Christ. Jesus has accomplished the task of breaking the authority of Satan and voiding his legal hold on the human race. Now my part as a believer is to exercise my God-given authority over Satan and the spiritual forces of evil.

Luke 10:18-19 **He [Jesus]** **replied, *"I saw Satan fall like lightning from heaven. I have given you authority to trample on snakes and scorpions and to overcome all the power of the enemy, nothing will harm you."*** I thank you Lord that you were there when Satan fell from the heavens to earth. Nothing gets past you O Lord. You Lord have also given me authority to trample on snakes and scorpions and to overcome all the power of the enemy. Not some of the power, part of the power but _all_ of the power. I trust you, nothing will harm me.

1 John 4:4 **You, dear children, are from God and have overcome them, because the one who is in you is greater than the one who is in the world.** I am from God. I am dear to him. I have already overcome evil spirits in him. The Holy Spirit in me is greater than Satan and all his demons and powers that are in the world. You are already defeated and overcome Satan. Greater are you Lord in me than <u>anything</u> in the world.

John 16:33b _**"But take heart! I have overcome the world."**_ Glory to you Lord, you have done it. I am encouraged. You have already overcome the evil of this present world. You have completed your work on the cross so that we may start from the place of victory.

John 16:11b _**"The prince of this world now stands condemned."**_ I praise you Jesus that Satan now stands condemned!

Ephesians 4:27 **And do not give the devil a foothold.** I give no place to the devil, he cannot take a place that I refuse to yield to him. Though he looks for some place to inhabit, I refuse any part of my body, soul, or spirit to him.

1 Corinthians 6:17 **But he who unites himself with the Lord is one with him in spirit.** I am one in spirit with the Lord, for I choose to

submit myself to him so that I may also be united with him.

James 4:7-8a **Submit yourselves, then, to God. Resist the devil, and he will flee from you. Come near to God and he will come near to you.** Right now I choose to submit and surrender myself wholly to God. I resist you Satan I oppose you and I stand against you. You must flee from me for I come near to my sweet Lord and he comes near to me.

1 Peter 5:8-9a **Be self-controlled and alert. Your enemy the devil prowls around like a roaring lion, looking for someone to devour. Resist him, standing firm in the faith.** I use self-control, I put the flesh down I am alert. I see my enemy prowling about, but he cannot devour me. I resist him standing firm in the faith, he has no power over me. I give him no place. My God makes me strong, firm and steadfast. I thank and praise God as I expectantly see his promises fulfilled in, for and to me. All power and glory be yours forever!

Revelation 12:11a **They overcame him by the blood of the Lamb and the word of their testimony.** We are in a very real war. Our weapons~ the name of Jesus, the blood of Jesus and our testimony of who God is and what he continues to do for us who believe, and the word of God. I too overcome Satan by the blood of the Lamb and the word of my testimony. As Jesus' blood availed for all on the cross and as the blood on the doorposts of the Israelites' houses caused the passover of judgment to spare them, I apply the blood to overcome all the power and warfare of the enemy. I plead the blood of Jesus over my body, my house, my home, my travels, my comings, my goings, my work, my school, my play, my family, friends, finances, ministry and my pets. I add to it the words of my testimony of God's goodness, his faithfulness, his power, his love and mercy. I overcome you Satan by the blood of the Lamb and the word of my testimony!

2 Corinthians 10:4-5 **The weapons we fight with are not the weapons of the world. On the contrary, they have divine power to demolish strongholds. We demolish arguments and every pretension that sets itself up against the knowledge of God, and we take captive every thought to make it obedient to Christ.** These weapons have divine power to not just tear down, but to totally demolish strongholds. I use these weapons to accomplish the work God intended them for. I demolish arguments and every spirit and pretension that sets itself up against the knowledge of God and I take captive every thought and line it up with the word, not paying attention to circumstances and feelings. I win the battle in him, both the battle in this world and the continual battles in my mind.

Colossians 2:15 **And having disarmed the powers and authorities, he made a public spectacle of them, triumphing over them by the cross.** Christ himself disarmed the powers and authorities that will come against me in this world. He triumphed over them by the cross, which can only mean that I too am coming from that place of victory!

Colossians 1:13-14 **For he has rescued us from the dominion of darkness and brought us into the kingdom of the Son he loves, in whom we have redemption, the forgiveness of sins.** Thank you, Father, that you have already delivered me from the power of darkness by Jesus' work on the cross, and that you have already brought me into the kingdom of your dear Son. I take my rightful place of authority over Satan and live in your kingdom right now.

Romans 16:20a **The God of peace will soon crush Satan under your feet.** I know you will do it Lord because you are the God of peace. I see Satan already, as crushed and under my feet.

Matthew 16:18b-19 *"On this rock I will build my church, and the gates of Hades will not overcome it. I will give you the keys of the kingdom of heaven, whatever you bind on earth will be bound in heaven and whatever you loose on earth will be loosed in heaven."* My confession of faith is that you Jesus are the Christ~ the Son of the living God. Thank you that you build your church on this confession of faith and that the gates of Hades and all the power of the enemy will not overcome it. Thank you for giving me the keys of the kingdom of heaven. Thank you that what I bind on earth, you bind in heaven and what I loose on earth, you loose in heaven. So in Jesus' name I bind [destruction, evil, sickness, deceit, darkness, strife, division, smallsightedness, etc.] on earth right now and in Jesus' name, I loose [light, restoration, strength, love, peace, joy, unity, truth, etc.] on earth to the honor and glory of God. Allelujah!

Hebrews 13:8 **Jesus Christ is the same yesterday and today and forever.** Thank you Jesus that you do not change, you do not say one thing today and change it tomorrow. You do not promise one thing in the Bible and take it away in this day and age. You are truly the same yesterday and today and forever. You are the same in love, power, compassion, mercy and character. Despite the constantly changing and threatening circumstances in this world, I know I can count on you. Thank-you Jesus!

Philippians 2:9-10 **Therefore God exalted him to the highest place and gave him the name that is above every name, that at the name of Jesus every knee should bow, in heaven and on earth and under the earth.** Father, I acknowledge with you that the name of Jesus is above every name, above everything in heaven, earth and hell. I choose to bow down to the name of Jesus even now, before the time of future glory when every knee will bow. I lift up the name of Jesus above all things, I put the name of Jesus in the highest place. I acknowledge Jesus as my Lord and Savior in every area of my life.

Ephesians 6:10-12, 14-18 **Finally, be strong in the Lord and in his mighty power. Put on the full armor of God so that you can take**

your stand against the devil's schemes. For our struggle is not against flesh and blood, but against the rulers, against the authorities, against the powers of this dark world, and against the spiritual forces of evil in the heavenly realms. Stand firm then, with the belt of truth buckled around your waist, with the breastplate of righteousness in place and with your feet fitted with the readiness that comes from the gospel of peace. In addition to all this, take up the shield of faith, with which you can extinguish all the flaming arrows of the evil one. Take the helmet of salvation and the sword of the Spirit, which is the word of God. And pray in the Spirit on all occasions with all kinds of prayers and requests. With this in mind, be alert and always keep on praying for all the saints.

I am strong in the Lord, I am strong in his mighty power, not my own. I put on the full armor of God, every piece and not just part of it and take my stand against every scheme of the devil. My struggle is not against flesh and blood, but against the rulers, authorities, powers, and spiritual forces of evil in the heavenlies. I keep my mind straight as to who the enemy is, I do not confuse the enemy as a mere person or people, but the power behind or within them. I stand my ground when the day of evil comes. After I have done everything I know to do, I solidly remain standing in faith believing God is able, willing and on my side. I stand firm with the belt of truth buckled around my waist, the Holy Spirit around me, in me, through me holding me up. My feet are perfectly fit and ready with the good news of peace. I take up the shield of faith with which I can extinguish all the flaming arrows of the evil one. I put on the breastplate of righteousness and the helmet of salvation, deliverance from Satan, sickness, need, confusion, fear and deliverance into eternal life in the future and the kingdom of God now. I take the sword of the Spirit which is God's own word and I speak it out boldly. Fully dressed and completely covered by the armor of God. I remain alert, ready and strong in the Lord.

Psalm 103:1-3 **Praise the LORD, O my soul, all my inmost being, praise his holy name. Praise the LORD, O my soul, and forget not all his benefits, who forgives all your sins and heals all your diseases.** Praise the LORD!

Greater Works Ministry 2006

A New Confession of Faith

So Jesus was saying to those Jews who had believed him, *"If you continue in my word, then you are truly disciples of mine: and you will know the truth, and the truth will make you free."* John 8:31-32 ~ I continue in your word, I am truly a disciple of yours, I will know the truth (Jesus) and the truth (Jesus) will make me free.

Finally, be strong in the Lord and in the strength of his might. Ephesians 6:10 ~ I am strong in the mighty strength of the LORD.

For I am confident of this very thing, that he who began a good work in you will perfect it until the day of Christ Jesus. Philippians 1:6 ~ I am confident that God, who began a good work in me, will finish, complete, end, perfect, attain the goal and undergo for me until the day of Christ Jesus.

The Lord is my Shepherd, I shall not want. Psalm 23:1 ~ The Lord is my Shepherd, I shall not be in want. I said~ I shall not be in want!

Fight the good fight of faith. 1 Timothy 6:12a ~ I fight the good fight of faith. A good fight is the one we win, Hallelujah!

And let us run with endurance the race that is set before us, fixing

our eyes on Jesus, the author and perfector of faith. Hebrews 12:1b-2a ~ I am running with endurance the race that is set before me, I am fixing my eyes on Jesus who is the author and perfector or finisher of faith.

I will instruct you and teach you in the way you should go, I will council you with my eye upon you. Psalm 32:8 ~ I am instructed and taught in the way I should go, I am counseled and God's eye is always upon me. Hallelujah!

Therefore humble yourselves under the mighty hand of God, that he may exalt you at the proper time, casting all your anxiety on him, because he cares for you. Be of sober *spirit*, be on the alert. Your adversary, the devil, prowls around like a roaring lion, seeking someone to devour. But resist him, firm in your faith, knowing that the same experiences of suffering are being accomplished by your brethren who are in the world. After you have suffered for a little while, the God of all grace, who called you to his eternal glory in Christ, will himself perfect, confirm, strengthen *and* establish you. To him *be* dominion forever and ever. Amen. 1 Peter 5:6-11 ~ I humble myself under God's mighty hand and he exalts me at the proper time. I cast all my anxiety on him because he cares for me. I am sober and alert because my enemy, the devil, is looking to devour me, I resist him in faith. I know others are experiencing the same trials and after suffering a little while, God himself will perfect, confirm, strengthen and establish me. To God alone, I give dominion forever and ever.

Now may the God of hope fill you with all joy and peace in believing, so that you will abound in hope by the power of the Holy Spirit. Romans 15:13 ~ Thank you God for filling me with all joy and peace as I believe, so that hope abounds in me by the power of the Holy Spirit.

L.A. Mars November 2007

The Power of the Tongue

Words are powerful! The LORD God spoke the world into being with his words. We must ask ourselves daily~ What are my words, powerful as they are, bringing into being?

Genesis 1:3 **And God <u>said</u>,** *"Let there be light," and there was light.*

Psalm 33:6 **By the <u>word</u> of the LORD were the heavens made, their starry host by the breath of his mouth.**

Psalm 33:9 **For he <u>spoke</u>, and it came to be, he <u>commanded</u>, and it stood firm.**

Hebrews 1:3a **The Son is the radiance of God's glory and the exact representation of his being, sustaining all things by his powerful <u>word</u>.**

Hebrews 11:3 **By faith we understand that the universe was formed at God's <u>command</u>, so that what is seen was not made out of what was visible.**

Romans 4:17b-24 **The God who gives life to the dead and <u>calls</u> things that be not as though they were. Against all hope, Abraham in hope believed and so became the father of many**

nations, just as it's been <u>said</u> to him, "So shall your offspring be". Without weakening in his faith, he faced the fact that his body was as good as dead– since he was about a hundred years old– and that Sarah's womb was also dead. Yet he did not waver through unbelief regarding the promise of God, but was strengthened in his faith and gave glory to God, being fully persuaded that God had power to do what he had promised. This is why "it was credited to him as righteousness." The <u>words</u> "it was credited to him" were written not for him alone, but also for us, to whom God will credit righteousness~ for us who believe in him who raised Jesus our Lord from the dead.

Our words also have the power to create, to bring about life and the substance of them when they are spoken in faith.

Proverbs 18:21 **The <u>tongue</u> has the power of life and death, and those who love it will eat its fruit.**

John 6:63b *The <u>words</u> I have <u>spoken</u> to you are spirit and they are life.*

Matthew 17:20b-21 *"I tell you the truth, if you have faith as small as a mustard seed, you can <u>say</u> to this mountain, 'Move from here to there' and it will move. Nothing will be impossible for you."*

Mark 11:22-26 *"Have faith in God," "I tell you the truth, if anyone <u>says</u> to this mountain, 'Go, throw yourself into the sea,' and does not doubt in his heart but believes that what he says will happen, it will be done for him. Therefore I tell you, whatever you <u>ask</u> for in prayer, believe that you have received it and it will be yours. And when you stand praying, if you hold anything against anyone, forgive him that your Father in heaven may forgive you your sins."*

James 3:2b-10 **If anyone is never at fault in what he <u>says</u>, he is a perfect man, able to keep his whole body in check. When we put bits into the mouths of horses to make them obey us, we can turn the whole animal. Or take ships as an example. Although they are so large and are driven by strong winds, they are steered by a very small rudder wherever the pilot wants to go. Likewise the <u>tongue</u> is a small part of the body, but it makes great boasts. Consider what a great forest is set on fire by a small spark. The <u>tongue</u> also is a fire, a world of evil among the parts of the body. It corrupts the whole person, sets the whole course of his life on fire, and is itself set on fire by hell. All kinds of animals, birds, reptiles and creatures of the sea are being tamed and have been tamed by man, but no man can tame the <u>tongue</u>. It is a restless evil, full of deadly poison. With the <u>tongue</u> we praise our Lord and Father, and with it we curse men who have been made in God's likeness. Out of the same <u>mouth</u> come praise and cursing. My brothers, this should not be.**

John 15:7 *"If you remain in me and my <u>words</u> remain in you, <u>ask</u> whatever you wish, and it will be given you."*

The Bible tells us to pay attention to God's words, to meditate on them day and night and to guard them in our hearts. It tells us they are life and health to our whole body!

Proverbs 4:20-22 **My son, pay attention to what I say, listen closely to my <u>words</u>. Do not let them out of your sight, keep them within your heart, for they are *life* to those who find them and *health* to a man's whole body**.

Joshua 1:8 **Do not let this Book of the Law depart from your <u>mouth</u>, meditate on it day and night, so that you may be careful to do everything in it. Then you will be prosperous and successful.**

Deuteronomy 6:6-9 **These commandments that I give you today are to be upon your hearts. Impress them on your children. <u>Talk</u> about them when you sit at home and when you walk along the road, when you lie down and when you get up. Tie them as symbols on your hands and bind them on your foreheads. Write them on the doorframes of your houses and on your gates**. Jesus himself says that we live by every word that proceeds from the mouth of God. So, what words are proceeding from your own mouth?

Matthew 4:4 Jesus said, *"It is written: 'Man does not live on bread alone, but on every <u>word</u> that comes from the mouth of God.'"*

We need to guard our words because they have consequences. Every word we speak should line up to the word of God.

Matthew 12:36-37 *"But I tell you that men will have to give account on the Day of Judgment for every careless <u>word</u> they have spoken. For by your <u>words</u> you will be acquitted and by your <u>words</u> you will be condemned."*

Numbers 14:17 **Now may the Lord's strength be displayed, just as you have <u>declared</u>.**

Numbers 14:28 **So tell them, as surely as I live <u>declares</u> the LORD, I will do to you the very things I heard you <u>say</u>.**

Isaiah 44:26a (I am the LORD) **who confirms the <u>word</u> of his servants and performs the <u>purpose</u> of his messengers.**

Luke 1:38a **"I am the Lord's servant," Mary answered. "May it be to me as you have <u>said</u>."** Mary said this after the angel told her that she would bear a child. "May it be to me as you have said Lord"!

Psalm 59:12-13 **For the sins of their <u>mouths</u>, for the <u>words</u> of their**

lips, let them be caught in their pride. For the curses and lies they utter, consume them in wrath till they are no more.

God tells us that our words reflect what is truly in our hearts. If we speak forth ugly words, _no matter what we tell ourselves,_ there is ugliness _(bitterness and unforgiveness)_ in our heart.

Matthew 12:34-35 *"You brood of vipers, how can you who are evil say anything good? <u>For out of the overflow of the heart,</u> <u>the mouth speaks.</u> The good man brings good things out of the good stored up in him, and the evil man brings evil things out of the evil stored up in him."*

Proverbs 6:16-19 **There are six things the LORD hates, seven that are detestable to him; haughty eyes, a lying <u>tongue</u>, hands that shed innocent blood, a heart that devises wicked schemes, feet that are quick to rush into evil, a false <u>witness</u> who pours out lies and a man who stirs up <u>dissension</u> among brothers.**

James 4:2b-3 **You do not have because you do not <u>ask</u> God. When you <u>ask</u>, you do not receive, because you <u>ask</u> with wrong motives, that you may spend what you get on your pleasures.**

Our words _can_ and should bring about positive things, like healing, truth and wisdom.

Proverbs 12:18-19 **Reckless <u>words</u> pierce like a sword, but the tongue of the wise brings healing. Truthful lips endure forever, but a lying <u>tongue</u> lasts only a moment.**

Proverbs 15:4 **The <u>tongue</u> that brings healing is a tree of life, but a deceitful <u>tongue</u> crushes the spirit.**

Luke 21:15 *"For I will give you <u>words</u> and wisdom that none of your adversaries will be able to resist or contradict."*

We are forgiven through our words of repentance. We must <u>ask</u> for forgiveness for our sins *before* our words can be heard by God.

Hosea 14:1-2 **Return, O Israel, to the LORD your God. Your sins have been your downfall! Take <u>words</u> with you and return to the LORD. <u>Say</u> to him, "Forgive all our sins and receive us graciously, that we may offer the fruit of our lips."**

James 1:19-21 **My dear brothers, take note of this: Everyone should be quick to listen, slow to <u>speak</u> and slow to become angry, for man's anger does not bring about the righteous life that God desires. Therefore, get rid of all moral filth and the evil that is so prevalent and humbly accept the <u>word</u> planted in you, which can save you.**

We always have a choice to exercise control over our tongues.

Psalm 17:3-4 **Though you probe my heart and examine me at night, though you test me, you will find nothing, I have resolved that my <u>mouth</u> will not sin. As for the deeds of men- by the <u>word</u> of your lips I have kept myself from the ways of the violent.**

Psalm 34:12-13 **Whoever of you loves life and desires to see many good days, keep your <u>tongue</u> from evil and your lips from <u>speaking</u> lies.**

Psalm 52:1-4 **Why do you boast of evil, you mighty man? Why do you boast all day long, you who are a disgrace in the eyes of God? Your <u>tongue</u> plots destruction, it is like a sharpened razor, you who practice deceit. You love evil rather than good, falsehood rather than <u>speaking</u> the truth. You love every harmful <u>word</u>, O you deceitful <u>tongue</u>!**

James 1:19b-20 **Everyone should be quick to listen, slow to <u>speak</u> and slow to become angry, for man's anger does not bring about the righteous life that God desires.**

Greater Works Ministries 2008

Confession: A Key to Unlocking Faith

Thoughts based on Ken Hagins' New Thresholds of Faith

Confession is a powerful tool of God. When some hear the word "confession" they think only of confessing shortcomings, sins, weaknesses or failings. This would only be the down or negative side of confession. There is a positive side of confession too that the bible has a lot to say about. The primary Greek word for "confess" is *homologeo* which basically means "to say the same thing" and then "agree, admit or acknowledge it."

The New Testament speaks of four different kinds of, or definitions of the word confession, let's look at these together.

1) The teachings of John the Baptist and Jesus regarding confession of sins by the Jews. **People went out to him** [John the Baptist] **from Jerusalem and all Judea and the whole region of the Jordan. Confessing their sins, they were baptized by him in the Jordan River.** Matthew 3:5-6

2) The confession of the sinner today.
But I tell you the truth: It is for your good that I am going away. Unless I go away the Counselor will not come to you, but if I go, I will send him to you. When he comes, he will convict the world of guilt in regard to sin and righteousness and judgment, in regard to

sin, because men do not believe in me; in regard to righteousness, because I am going to the Father, where you can see me no longer; and in regard to judgment, because the prince of this world now stands condemned. John 16:7-11

3) The believer's confession when he is out of fellowship with God.
This is the message we have heard from him and declare to you; God is light, in him there is no darkness at all. If we claim to have fellowship with him yet walk in the darkness, we lie and do not live by the truth. But if we walk in the light, as he is in the light, we have fellowship with one another, and the blood of Jesus, his Son, purifies us from all sin. If we claim to be without sin, we deceive ourselves and the truth is not in us. If we confess our sins, he is faithful and just and will forgive us our sins and purify us from all unrighteousness. If we claim we have not sinned, we make him out to be a liar and his word has no place in our lives.
1 John 1:5-10

4) The confession of our faith in God and God's Word.
That if you confess with your mouth, "Jesus is Lord" and believe in your heart that God raised him from the dead, you will be saved. For it is with your heart that you believe and are justified and it is with your mouth that you confess and are saved.
Romans 10:9-10

God wants our confession to be public, that is, to other men. This indicates a break with the world. It defines our position by showing a change of Lordship. The confession of the Lordship of Jesus puts us immediately under his supervision, care and protection. We confess to men, to God and to Satan the Lordship of the risen Christ. In this way we overcome the world and the devil and have victory through Jesus.

"Whoever acknowledges me before men, I will acknowledge him before my Father in heaven. But whoever disowns me before men, I will disown him before my Father in heaven." Matthew 10:32-33

What does Confession look like?

1) **Confession preaches the word.**

"Go into all the world and preach the good news to all creation. Whoever believes and is baptized will be saved, but whoever does not believe will be condemned. And these signs will accompany those who believe: In my name they will drive out demons; they will speak in new tongues; they will pick up snakes with their hands; and when they drink deadly poison, it will not hurt them at all; they will place their hands on sick people, and they will get well." After the Lord Jesus had spoken to them, he was taken up into heaven and he sat at the right hand of God. Then the disciples went out and preached everywhere and the Lord worked with them and confirmed his word by the signs that accompanied it. Mark 16:15-20

The Holy Spirit works in connection with the preaching of the word. In obedience to Jesus' command to go into all the world and preach, the disciples went forth preaching and the Lord worked with them confirming the word with signs following. God allowed the disciples to preach, then signs followed. Signs don't follow an individual, they follow the preaching (the speaking) of the word. Speak the word out and the signs will take care of themselves. If the signs aren't following, maybe you're not preaching the word. The less you preach tradition and personal opinion and the more you preach the undiluted word of God the more you will see signs following.

2) **Confessions Dispel Fear**
So do not fear, for I am with you; do not be dismayed, for I am your God. I will strengthen you and help you, I will uphold you with my righteous right hand. Isaiah 41:10

"Don't be afraid, just believe and she will be healed." Luke 8:50

Do we really believe he's with us, strengthening and helping us if we are still afraid? Fear usually indicates doubt. The scriptures tell us to cast off fear and look to the word for strength. **My soul is weary with sorrow, strengthen me according to your word.** Psalm 119:28 ~ **The unfolding of your words gives light, it gives understanding to the simple.** Psalm 119:130

Instead of talking about difficulties and impossibilities, speak the word. **~ Greater is he that is in me than he that is in the world.** 1 John 4:4b ~ Speak to your problem and tell it how big and able your God is. **If God be for us, who can be against us?** Romans 8:31 ~ As you speak positive confessions of faith, your fears will and must flee before the truth.

3) Confessions Increase Faith

Confession is the way faith expresses itself. Faith, like love, is of the heart and of the spirit. We know there is no love without word or action. We cannot reason love into people, nor can we reason it out of them, it's a matter of the heart. Faith also is of the heart, like love, we can neither reason it into us or reason it out of us.

The confession of the believer identifies them and sets the boundaries for their life. One reason many Christians, although sincere, are weak is because they have not made a confession of whom and what they are in Christ. We must find out how God looks at us and then confess it. Your daily confession of what the Father is to you, of what Jesus is doing for you right now and of what the Holy Spirit is doing in you will build a solid, positive faith life. You will not fear circumstances, disease, lack or conditions. **No, in all these things we are more than conquerors through him who loved us.** Romans 8:37

You will face life fearlessly as a conqueror when you confess who you are in Christ and who he is in you. In seeking anything from God, you must first believe it in your heart because the word says it, next we must confess it with our mouths. *I tell you the truth, if anyone says to this mountain, 'Go, throw yourself into the sea,' and does not doubt in his heart but believes that what he says will happen, it will be done for him.* Mark 11:23 In doing so you will begin to see that in one sense, faith's confession creates reality. It is always possible to tell if a person is believing right by what he says. If his confession is wrong, his believing is wrong. If his believing is wrong, his thinking is wrong. If his thinking is wrong, it is because his mind has not been renewed with the word of God. Believing, thinking and saying all go together.

Confession is stating something we believe in our hearts. It gives evidence to something we know is true, something we accept as truth.

Our positive confession of faith should center around 5 things~
    1) What God has done for us in the plan of redemption.
    2) What God has done in us through his word and his Spirit.
    3) What God can accomplish through us.
    4) What we are to the Father in Christ.
    5) What Jesus is accomplishing for us now at the Father's right hand where he makes intercession for us.

Confession then, is simply testifying to something we know. First, we can come to know him personally~ it's only through his word that we can truly discover who and what we are and have in Christ.

Therefore, if anyone is in Christ, he is a new creation, the old has gone, the new has come! 2 Corinthians 5:17 ~ From this verse we learn that when we are born again, we're new creations in Christ and that the old has gone and the new has come! Hallelujah!

Our desires and interests change as we confess this truth. We learn that we are redeemed from the curse of the law. **Christ redeemed us from the curse of the law by becoming a curse for us.** Galatians 3:13a ~ We learn that the curse included sickness and poverty in Deuteronomy 28:15-69. We learn that we are delivered from the power of Satan~ **For he has rescued us from the dominion of darkness and brought us into the kingdom of the Son he loves.** Colossians 1:13 ~ **You, dear children, are from God and have overcome them, because the one who is in you is greater than the one who is in the world.** 1 John 4:4 ~ To speak true confessions, we must get our thinking in line with God's word. It is then that our believing will be right. Only then will we be able to confess [say, affirm, witness and testify] to what God's word says about us. This in and of itself is where our success will spring forth from.

Right Confession and Wrong Confession

The confession of our lips will give God or Satan dominion over us. **For God hath not given us the spirit of fear, but a spirit of power and of love and of a sound mind.** 2 Timothy 1:7

He himself bore our sins in his body on the tree, so that we might die to sins and live for righteousness, by his wounds you have been healed. 1 Peter 2:24

He took up our infirmities and carried our diseases. Matthew 8:17

The word of God, the bible, contains God's thoughts which are way different than ours. **For my thoughts are not your thoughts, neither are your ways my ways, declares the LORD. As the heavens are higher than the earth, so are my ways higher than your ways and my thoughts than your thoughts.** Isaiah 55:8-9

Sometimes the teaching of the word of God may not seem reasonable to the natural man, that's only because his mind has not been renewed by the word. Our intellect and physical senses will fight us every step of the way to keep us from entering into the spiritual realm and keep us in the natural realm. Wrong confession is a confession of defeat, failure and the supremacy of Satan and it will keep us in bondage and defeat. Right confession is when we testify to what God has done for us and it glorifies him. Any confession that glorifies Satan is an unconscious declaration that God is a failure. Therefore, with your mouth you either give God or you give Satan dominion over you. The confession of your lips that has grown out of faith in your heart based on what the word says, will absolutely defeat the devil as you resist him with the word. It's God's word that gives you the victory! Amen.

When Satan has dominion over us, we are deceived and filled with his weakness and fear. When God has dominion, he fills us with power, love and a sound mind. Fear is not something that comes from the inside you. It's something that comes from the outside of you that's trying to get hold of you. It comes from the enemy and the same is true of doubt. When you confess doubts, the enemy is speaking. Many people think they are being honest when they confess their doubts. The word says to resist the devil and he will flee from you. **Submit yourselves then to God. Resist the devil and he will flee from you.** James 4:7 ~ Refuse to doubt. Confess faith. Start talking about who you are and what you are in Christ, a believer, a new creature, a child of God, a person with a spirit of power, love and a sound mind, not a doubter or fearer. Confess your Father's care and protection, his word and that what he says about you is true, that he is greater in you than Satan is in this world, that you will rise above satanic influence and walk in victory because of what Christ has done for you. Amen.

Greater Works Ministries 2008

Marriage Warfare

According to your word, Matthew 19:6 says: **So they are no longer two, but one. Therefore what God has joined together, let man** [nor Satan] **not separate.** _____ and I are one. I thank you Father that it's your will that the two of us are one. Lord I thank you for a breaking of the strife that has had its hold on us, take away the armor I have erected to protect myself, for you alone are my protector. Tear down this wall between us and enable me to rise up from the rubble and live in the oneness you have for us. For you alone are my hope. I ask you Father to speak through me so that my words reflect your love, peace, joy and reconciliation.

Father I confess my unforgiveness, anger, hurt, hatred, loveless-ness, disappointment, resentment, hardheartedness, suspicions, accusations and contempt towards _____. I also confess that these thoughts and attitudes towards him are also sin against you, please lift me out of the pit of despair. Will you please forgive me and in Jesus name deliver me and purify me from all unrighteousness. Father, I need a new positive, joyful, loving and forgiving attitude towards _____. I can only love him this way through you, please enable me to do so this day. Help me to maintain a home (heart) that is pleasing for him to come into.

Father though it seems safer to hang onto some of these feelings, I realize that when I am doing this, I am not trusting you. You have promised that I can trust you and I want to do what you want me to do, please give me a renewed sense of love for him and words to heal situations so I may be pleasing unto you. Lord, show me when to be silent and show me when to speak, please set a guard over my tongue and lips. I confess that at times I have shown a lack of respect towards _____ and do not esteem him as you command in your word to. I confess that my disrespectful attitude and words are sin against him and you. Show me how to dismantle this barrier over my emotions that keep me from having the unconditional love towards _____ you desire for me to have. Tear down the hardness of heart and show me how to respect _____ the way you want me to.

Please give me your heart for him and enable me to see him the way you see him. Help me to not hold myself apart from him emotionally, mentally, physically or spiritually because of my feelings. Instead I ask that you would give me insight into what causes him to shut down and how I can appropriately respond to bring your peace to the situation. If there is something I am not seeing that is adding to the problem, reveal it to me and help me understand it so that no wedge would come between us. Where there are behaviors that need to change in either of us I pray you would enable that change to happen.

In Jesus name I will not allow anything to destroy my marriage, I will not sit by while walls go up between us; I will not allow confusion, miscommunication, wrong attitudes or bad choices to erode what we are building together. I will not tolerate hurt feelings. According to Mathew 18:18 – you Father have given me authority in Jesus name to bind these things, so Father, I submit to you and bind in Jesus name all these things that I perceive control _____- [work, TV, anger, addiction, anxiety, lack of purpose, fear of failure and pride]. I command in Jesus name that he be loosed from these and a desire for you and your word to fill that void! Father where _____ has erred, reveal it to him and convict his heart about it. I pray your voice would penetrate _____ soul and that you would lead him through the paths of repentance and deliverance so that he walks in victory! I pray he discovers his purpose in you. May he always be well paid for the work he does. I pray that your storehouse of blessings will be poured out upon him. _____ is a believer and he takes good care of our home. He goes to church, he loves me and he loves his family. He reads his bible, he has high moral standards and he uses his talents for your glory. He is a good and generous provider, he is intellectual yet funny and he takes good care of himself! He loves children and he loves animals too. Thank you Father for such a wonderful man! His divine power has given us everything we need for life and godliness through our knowledge of him who called us by his own glory and goodness. 2 Peter 1:3

The prayer above is based upon the book *"The power of a praying wife"* by Stormie O'Martian

L.A. Mars October 2008

Jesus You Are

Jesus you are my Savior
Jesus you are my Protector
Jesus you are my Defender
Jesus you are my Lord, my Lord of Lords
Jesus you are my King, and King of Kings
Jesus you are my Righteousness
Jesus you are my Forgiveness
Jesus you are my Breath
Jesus you are my Rock
Jesus you are my Fortress
Jesus you are my All
Jesus you are my Love
Jesus you are my Healer
Jesus you are my Bread
Jesus you are my Hope
Jesus you are my Prince of Peace
Jesus you are my Plans
Jesus you are my Purpose
Jesus you are my Joy
Jesus you are my Patience
Jesus you are my Wisdom
Jesus you are my Knowledge
Jesus you are my Guide
Jesus you are my Shepherd
Jesus you are my Gentleness
Jesus you are my Teacher
Jesus you are my Revelator
Jesus you are my Way
Jesus you are my Light
Jesus you are my Brother
Jesus you are my Freedom

Jesus you are my Salvation
Jesus you are my Truth
Jesus you are my Strength
Jesus you are my Friend
Jesus you are my Kindness
Jesus you are my Goodness
Jesus you are my Gentleness
Jesus you are my Counselor
Jesus you are my Desire
Jesus you are my Fire
Jesus you are my Comforter
Jesus you are my Perfector
Jesus you are my Redemption
Jesus you are my Assurance
Jesus you are my Grace
Jesus you are my Provision
Jesus you are my Courage
Jesus you are my Eternity
Jesus you are my Praise
Jesus you are my Song
Jesus you are my Life
Jesus you are my Priest
Jesus you are my Strong tower
Jesus you are my Shield
Jesus you are my Restorer
Jesus you are my Self control
Jesus you are my Satisfaction
Jesus you are my Mercy
Jesus you are everything I'm not
Jesus you are everything I want to be
Jesus you are my All in All

L.A. Mars April 2006

Daily Prayer

Heavenly Father, I come to you this day to worship and give you thanks. I thank you for sleep and for being able to see, hear, smell, feel, taste and move this day. I am blessed because you are a faithful, understanding and forgiving God. You have done so much for me~ then you just keep on doing it and blessing me more!

Father, I know you have forgiven me, restored me and I know you guide me. I ask for your protection this day and that you would deliver me from all danger and harm. I plead the blood of Jesus over our bodies, our house, our home, our travels, our comings and goings our work, our school, our play, our family, our friends, our finances, ministries and our pets. Father I ask that you renew my strength this day so that all I think, say or do would be pleasing unto you. May my attitude be full of gratitude and praise toward you. I pray that my mind and heart will be fixed on you as you open the eyes of my heart so that I may hear from you.

Holy Spirit, convict me when I whimper or whine especially over the things out of my control and may I repent quickly and turn back to you Lord. When the world seems to be closing in on me remind me of Jesus' example to slip away and find a quiet place to pray. I know that the Holy Spirit intercedes on my behalf and I know that you see every tear that falls. Father use me this day to further your kingdom, to bless others, to pray for those in need and to lend a word of encouragement where it's needed. May it be so. I pray for those who don't yet know you and for those who have strayed from the faith. I lift up those who are lost and cannot seem to find there way, draw them unto yourself Father as only you can and remove the veil of deception from their eyes so that they would turn and be saved.

For those who are misguided, misjudged or misunderstood~ I pray for endurance. I pray for our family and neighbors, Lord bless their homes, their hearts and jobs. I pray for debt free households and that homes would be full of your love, joy and peace.

Lord I believe that you are the changer of hearts and lives and I thank you for continually changing mine! I praise you Lord that my needs are met. I thank you Lord that you hear my prayers! I love you Lord, I now commit this day into your loving hands and it's in the mighty name of Jesus that I pray. Amen!

L.A. Mars

Assurance

And my God will meet all your needs according to his glorious riches in Christ Jesus. Philippians 4:19

Commit to the LORD whatever you do and your plans will succeed. Proverbs 16:3

The Lord is my Shepherd, I shall not be in want. Psalm 23:1

Praise be to the Lord, to God our Savior, who daily bears our burdens. Psalm 68:19

Cast your cares on the LORD and he will sustain you. Psalm 55:22a

Jesus answered, "It is written: 'man does not live on bread alone, but on every word that comes from the mouth of God.'" Matthew 4:4

But seek first his kingdom and his righteousness, and all these things will be given to you as well. Matthew 6:33

Cast all your anxiety on him because he cares for you. 1 Peter 5:7

Fear the LORD, you his saints, for those who fear him lack nothing. Psalm 34:9

I will instruct you and teach you in the way you should go, I will council you and watch over you. Proverbs 32:8

Misfortune pursues the sinner, but prosperity is the reward of the righteous. Proverbs 13:21

But those who seek the LORD lack no good thing. Psalm 34:10b

Trust in the LORD with all your heart and lean not on your own understanding; in all your ways acknowledge him, and he will make your paths straight. Proverbs 3:5-6

Consider it pure joy, my brothers, whenever you face trials of many kinds, because you know that the testing of your faith develops perseverance. Perseverance must finish its work so that you may be mature and complete, not lacking anything. If any of you lacks wisdom, he should ask God, who gives generously to all without finding fault, and it will be given to him. James 1:2-5

Do not be anxious about anything, but in everything, by prayer and petition, with thanksgiving, present your requests to God.
Philippians 4:6

And we know that in all things God works for the good of those who love him, who have been called according to his purpose.
Romans 8:28

For I know the plans I have for you declares the LORD, "plans to prosper you, and not to harm you, plans to give you a hope and a future. Jeremiah 29:11

L.A. Mars March 2006

Healing & Refreshment

Proverbs 3:1-8

My son, do not forget my teaching

It will be healing to your body and refreshment to your bones.

Do not let kindness and truth leave you

It will be healing to your body and refreshment to your bones.

Trust in the Lord with all your heart

It will be healing to your body and refreshment to your bones.

In all your ways, acknowledge him

It will be healing to your body and refreshment to your bones.

Do not be wise in your own eyes

It will be healing to your body and refreshment to your bones.

~~~~~~~~~~~~~~~~~~~~~

1) My son, do not forget my teaching

It will be healing to your body and refreshment to your bones.

But let your heart keep my commandments.

2) For length of days and years of life

It will be healing to your body and refreshment to your bones.

And peace they will add to you.

3) Do not let kindness and truth leave you

It will be healing to your body and refreshment to your bones.

Bind them around your neck, write them on the tablet of your heart

It will be healing to your body and refreshment to your bones.

4) So you will find favor and good repute in the sight of God and man

It will be healing to your body and refreshment to your bones.

5) Trust in the Lord with all your heart

It will be healing to your body and refreshment to your bones.

And do not lean on your own understanding.

It will be healing to your body and refreshment to your bones.

6) In all your ways acknowledge him

It will be healing to your body and refreshment to your bones.

And he will make your paths straight.

7) Do not be wise in your own eyes

It will be healing to your body and refreshment to your bones.

Fear the LORD and turn away from evil.

It will be healing to your body and refreshment to your bones.

8) It will be healing to your body and refreshment to your bones.

L.A. Mars June 2008

In Christ

Romans 3:22-24 This righteousness from God comes through faith <u>in Jesus Christ</u> to all who believe. There is no difference, for all have sinned and fall short of the glory of God and are justified freely by his grace through the redemption that came by Christ Jesus.

Romans 5:11 Not only is this so, but we also rejoice <u>in God through our Lord Jesus Christ</u>, through whom we have now received reconciliation.

Romans 6:23 For the wages of sin is death, but the gift of God is eternal life <u>in Christ Jesus our Lord</u>.

Romans 8:1-2 Therefore, there is now no condemnation for those who are <u>in Christ Jesus</u>, because through Christ Jesus the law of the Spirit of life set me free from the law of sin and death.

Romans 9:1a I speak the truth <u>in Christ</u>...

Romans 12:4-5 Just as each of us has one body with many members, and these members do not all have the same function, so <u>in Christ</u> we who are many form one body and each member belongs to all the others.

Romans 16:3, 7, 9-10 Greet Pricilla and Aquila, my fellow workers <u>in Christ Jesus</u>. Greet Andronicus and Junias, my relatives who have been in prison with me. They are outstanding among the apostles, and they were <u>in Christ</u> before I was. Greet Apelles, tested and approved <u>in Christ</u>.

1 Corinthians 1:2 To the church of God in Corinth, to those sanctified <u>in Christ</u> and called to be holy, together with all those everywhere who call on the name of our Lord Jesus Christ- their Lord and ours.

1 Corinthians 1:30 It is because of him that you are <u>in Christ Jesus</u>, who has become for us wisdom from God- that is, our righteousness,

holiness and redemption.

1 Corinthians 4:10 We are fools for Christ, you are so wise <u>in Christ!</u>

1 Corinthians 4:15 Even though you have ten thousand guardians <u>in Christ</u>, you do not have many fathers, for <u>in Christ</u> I became your father through the gospel.

1 Corinthians 4:17 For this reason I am sending to you Timothy, my son whom I love, who is faithful in the Lord. He will remind you of my way of life <u>in Christ Jesus</u>, which agrees with what I teach everywhere in every church.

1 Corinthians 15:19 If only for this life we have hope <u>in Christ</u>, we are to be pitied more than all men.

1 Corinthians 15:22 For as in Adam all die, so <u>in Christ</u> all will be made alive.

1 Corinthians 16:24 My love to all of you <u>in Christ Jesus</u>.

2 Corinthians 1:21-22 Now it is God who makes both us and you stand firm <u>in Christ</u>. He anointed us, he set his seal of ownership on us, and he put his Spirit in our hearts as a deposit, guaranteeing what is to come.

2 Corinthians 2:14 But thanks be to God, who always leads us in triumphal procession in Christ and through us spreads everywhere the fragrance of the knowledge of him.

2 Corinthians 2:17 Unlike so many, we do not peddle the word of God for profit. On the contrary, <u>in Christ</u> we speak before God with sincerity, like men sent from God.

2 Corinthians 3:14 But their minds were made dull, for to this day the same veil remains when the old covenant is read. It has not been removed, because only <u>in Christ</u> is it taken away.

2 Corinthians 12:19b We have been speaking in the sight of God as those in Christ, and everything we do dear friends is for your strengthening.

2 Corinthians 5:17 Therefore, if anyone is in Christ, he is a new creation, the old is gone, the new has come!

Galatians 1:22-24 I was personally unknown to the churches of Judea that are in Christ. They only heard the report: "The man who formerly persecuted us is now preaching the faith he once tried to destroy. And they praised God because of me.

Galatians 2:4 This matter arose because some false brothers had infiltrated our ranks to spy on the freedom we have in Christ and to make us slaves.

Galatians 2:15-16 We who are Jews by birth and not 'Gentile sinners' know that a man is not justified by observing the law, but by faith in Jesus Christ. So we, too, have put our faith in Christ Jesus that we may be justified by faith in Christ and not by observing the law, because by observing the law no one will be justified.

Galatians 3:26 You are all sons of God through faith in Christ Jesus.

Ephesians 1:3-14 Praise be to the God and Father of our Lord Jesus Christ, who has blessed us in the heavenly realms with every spiritual blessing in Christ. For he chose us in him before the creation of the world to be holy and blameless in his sight. In love he predestined us to be adopted as his sons through Jesus Christ, in accordance with his pleasure and will- to the praise of his glorious grace, which he has freely given us in the One he loves. In him [Christ] we have redemption through his blood, the forgiveness of sins, in accordance with the riches of God's grace that he lavished on us with all wisdom and understanding. And he made known to us the mystery of his will according to his good pleasure, which he purposed in Christ, to be put into effect when times will have reached their fulfillment- to bring all things in heaven and on earth together under one head, even Christ. In him [Christ] we were also chosen, having been predestined according to the plan of him who works out everything in conformity with the purpose of his will, in order that we, who were the first to hope in Christ, might be for the praise of his glory. And you also were included in Christ when you heard the word of truth, the gospel of your salvation. Having believed you were marked in him [Christ] with a seal, the promised Holy Spirit, who is a deposit guaranteeing our inheritance until the redemption of those who are God's possession- to the praise of his glory.

Ephesians 1:18-20 I pray also that the eyes of your heart may be enlightened in order that you may know the hope to which he has called you, the riches of his glorious inheritance in the saints, and his incomparably great power for us who believe. That power is like the working of his mighty strength, which he exerted in Christ when he raised him from the dead and seated him at his right hand in the heavenly realms.

Ephesians 2:6-7 And God raised us up with Christ and seated us with him in the heavenly realms in Christ Jesus, in order that in the coming ages he might show the incomparable riches of his grace, expressed in his kindness to us in Christ Jesus.

Ephesians 2:10 For we are God's workmanship, created in Christ Jesus to do good works, which God prepared in advance for us to do.

Ephesians 2:13 But now in Christ Jesus you who once were far away have been brought near through the blood of Christ.

Ephesians 3:6 This mystery is that through the gospel the Gentiles are heirs together with Israel, members together of one body, and sharers together in the promise in Christ Jesus.

Ephesians 3:10-12 His intent was that now, through the church, the manifold wisdom of God should be made known to the rulers and authorities in the heavenly realms, according to his eternal purpose which he accomplished in Christ Jesus our Lord. In him [Christ] and through faith <u>in him</u> [Christ] we may approach God with freedom and confidence.

Ephesians 4:32 Be kind and compassionate to one another, forgiving each other, just as <u>in Christ</u> God forgave you.

Philippians 1:1 To all the saints <u>in Christ</u> Jesus at Philippi, together with the overseers and deacons.

Philippians 3:3 For it is we who are the circumcision, we who worship by the Spirit of God, who glory <u>in Christ Jesus</u> and who put no confidence in the flesh.

Philippians 3:14 I press on toward the goal to win the prize for which God has called me heavenward <u>in Christ Jesus.</u>

Philippians 4:19 And my God will meet all your needs according to his glorious riches <u>in Christ Jesus.</u>

Colossians 1:3-4 We always thank God, the Father of our Lord Jesus Christ, when we pray for you, because we have heard of your faith <u>in Christ Jesus</u> and of your love you have for all the saints.

Colossians 1:28 We proclaim him, admonishing and teaching every-one with all wisdom, that we may present everyone perfect <u>in Christ.</u>

Colossians 2:5 For though I am absent from you in body, I am present with you in spirit and delight to see how orderly you are and how firm your faith <u>in Christ</u> is.

Colossians 3:3 For you died and your life is now hidden with <u>Christ in God.</u>

Colossians 2:9-11a For <u>in Christ</u> all the fullness of the Deity lives in bodily form and you have been given fullness <u>in Christ,</u> who is the head over every power and authority. <u>In him</u> [Christ] you were also circumcised in the putting off of the sinful nature.

Colossians 2:17 These are a shadow of the things that were to come; the reality, however, is found in Christ.

1 Thessalonians 1:3 We continually remember before our God and Father your work produced by faith, your labor prompted by love, and your endurance inspired by hope in our Lord Jesus Christ.

1 Thessalonians 2:14a For you brothers, became imitators of God's churches in Judea, which are in Christ Jesus.

1 Thessalonians 4:16 We believe that Jesus died and rose again and so we believe that God will bring with Jesus those who have fallen asleep in him. [Christ] *(We will see them again!)* ***Hallelujah!***

1 Thessalonians 5:18 Give thanks in all circumstances, for this is God's will for you in Christ Jesus.

1 Timothy 1:14 The grace of our Lord was poured out on me abundantly, along with the faith and love that are in Christ.

1 Timothy 3:13 Those who have served well gain an excellent standing and great assurance in their faith in Christ Jesus.

2 Timothy1:1 Paul, an apostle of Christ Jesus by the will of God, according to the promise of life that is in Christ Jesus.

2 Timothy 1:9b This grace was given us in Christ Jesus before the beginning of time.

2 Timothy 1:13 What you heard from me, keep as the pattern of sound teaching, with faith and love in Christ Jesus.

2 Timothy 2:1 You then, my son, be strong in the grace that is in Christ Jesus.

2 Timothy 2:10 Therefore I endure everything for the sake of the elect, that they too may obtain the salvation that is <u>in Christ Jesus</u>, with eternal Glory.

2 Timothy 3:12 In fact, everyone who wants to live a godly life <u>in Christ Jesus</u> will be persecuted.

2 Timothy 3:14-15 But as for you, continue in what you have learned and have become convinced of, because you know those from whom you have learned it, and how from infancy you have known the holy scriptures, which are able to make you wise for salvation through faith <u>in Christ Jesus</u>.

Philemon 1:6 I pray that you may be active in sharing your faith, so that you will have a full understanding of every good thing we have <u>in Christ</u>.

Philemon 1:8-9 Therefore, although <u>in Christ</u> I could be bold and order you to do what you ought to do, yet I appeal to you on the basis of love.

Philemon 1:23 Epaphras, my fellow prisoner <u>in Christ Jesus</u>, sends you greetings. And so do Mark, Aristarchus, Demas and Luke, my fellow workers.

L.A. Mars July 2006

I Forbid…

I put these one liner confessions together to defeat sickness in my body. I repeated them for a couple of years on a daily basis, not wavering but holding to the truth until it got deep down into my soul. I put a copy in my bible, I kept one in the kitchen, also at my desk so that when the enemy started speaking I could remind myself and him who my Lord and Savior is and what my inheritance in Christ includes! I encourage you to do the research to find the scriptures you need for the season of trials you are facing right now. I pray you will begin speaking them forth from your own mouth! Amen.

In Jesus name I forbid sickness to be in my body!

Healing and wholeness is my inheritance!

I demand my full rights in Jesus name!

It's been paid for!

Healing is mine, it belongs to me!

I will not come short of God's glory!

You are a defeated foe Satan, so flee!

He himself bore my sins…

By his stripes I was healed!

No weapon formed against me shall prevail!

I walk by faith, not by sight!

I am a child of the Most High God!

I am a temple of the Holy Spirit!

I have been redeemed from the curse of the law!

This is not mine, I am not taking it- take your hands off of me!

God's word works!

I submit to the Lord, resist the devil and he flees from me!

Greater is he who is in me than he who is in the world!

No, in all these things I am more than a conqueror!

All authority in heaven and on earth has been given to me!

The prince of this world now stands condemned!

I am the righteousness of God in Christ Jesus!

I am his workmanship!

He has rescued me from the dominion of darkness!

I am the head and not the tail!

I thank you that I am in right standing with you
because of Jesus' work on the cross!

Jesus reigns in my life!

Halleluiah!

Oh God, be glorified in my body!

Hallelujah! Hallelujah! Hallelujah!

With God on my side, I cannot be defeated, God is with me,
he is for me and if God is for me, who then can be against me!

Hallelujah!

L.A. Mars November 2008

Satan ~ I rebuke you!

By his stripes I was healed.

No weapon forged against me shall prevail.

I am strong in the mighty strength of the Lord.

I have the mind of Christ.

I have not been given a spirit of fear,

but a spirit of power, love and self discipline.

According to God's word, I am healed.

I'm fighting off this attack in my body.

We've all been given a measure of faith.

I can do all things through Christ who strengthens me.

I will live and not die and proclaim the works of the Lord.

I walk by faith, not by sight.

I am a child of the Most High God.

I am a temple of the Holy Spirit.

I have been redeemed from the curse of the law.

This is not mine (sickness) I'm not taking it,

Satan, you take your hands off of me.

I submit to the Lord, I resist the devil and he flees from me.

Satan, you're a liar, I don't believe you,

I believe God and his word.

God's word works!

Ask and it shall be given.

I lay my hands on the sick and see them recover.

Greater is he who is in me than he who is in the world.

My God shall supply all my needs according
to his riches in Christ Jesus.

I take captive every thought to make it obedient to Christ.

In all these things we are more than conquerors.

The Lord is my Shepherd I shall not be in want.

All authority in heaven and on earth has been given to me.

The prince of this world now stands condemned.

For he has rescued us from the dominion of darkness.

O Lord my God, I called to you for help and you healed me.

The Lord will rescue me from every evil attack.

He himself bore my sins…

Praise be to the God and Father of our Lord Jesus Christ
who has rescued us from every evil attack.

Cast your burden on the LORD and he will sustain you. Psalm 55:22a

But you, O LORD, are a shield about me, my glory
and the one who lifts my head. Psalm 3:3

Make me know your ways O LORD, teach me your paths.
Lead me in your truth and teach me, for you are the God of my
salvation. For you I wait all the day. Psalm 25:4-5

L.A. Mars August 2006

Trust In Him

I am not adequate in myself, my adequacy comes from the LORD.
2 Corinthians 3:5 His adequacy is in me! Hallelujah!!!

Establish your word to your servant, as that which produces reverence for you. Psalm 119:38

And those who know your name will put their trust in you, for you, O LORD have not forsaken those who seek you. Psalm 9:10

I love you O LORD my strength. The LORD is my rock and my fortress and my deliverer, my God, my rock in whom I take refuge; my shield and the horn of my salvation, my stronghold. I call upon the LORD who is worthy to be praised and I am saved from my enemies. 2 Samuel 22:2-4, Psalm 18:1-3

To you, O LORD, I lift up my soul. O my God, in you I trust, do not let me be ashamed; do not let my enemies exult over me.
Psalm 25:1-2

The LORD is my strength and shield, my heart trusts in him and I am helped; therefore my heart exults, and with my song I shall thank him.
Psalm 28:7

O taste and see that the LORD is good, how blessed is the man who takes refuge in him! Psalm 34:8

The LORD redeems the soul of his servants and none of those who take refuge {trust} in him will be condemned. Psalm 34:22

Trust in the LORD and do good, dwell in the land and cultivate faithfulness. Delight yourself in the LORD and he will give you the desires of your heart. Commit your way to the LORD, trust also in him and he will do it. Psalm 37:3-5

Behold, God is my helper; the LORD is the sustainer of my soul. He will recompense the evil to my foes, destroy them in your faithfulness. Psalm 54:4-5

When I am afraid I will put my trust in you. In God I have put my trust, I shall not be afraid. What can mere man do to me?
Psalm 56:3-4, 11

Trust in the LORD with all your heart and do not lean on your own understanding. In all your ways acknowledge him and he will make your paths straight. Do not be wise in your own eyes, fear the LORD and turn away from evil. It will be healing to your body and refreshment to your bones. Proverbs 3:5-8

An arrogant man stirs up strife, but he who trusts in the LORD will prosper. He who trusts in his own heart is a fool, but he who walks wisely will be delivered. Proverbs 28:25-26

Every word of God is tested, he is a shield to those who take refuge {trust} in him. Proverbs 30:5

The steadfast of mind you will keep in perfect peace, because he trusts in you. Trust in the LORD forever, for in God the LORD, we have an everlasting Rock. Isaiah 26:3-4

Trust God from the bottom of your heart
and don't try to figure everything out on your own.
Listen for God's voice in everything you do, everywhere you go,
he's the one who will keep you on track.
Proverbs 3:6 TM

L.A. Mars September 2009

Ephesians 3:14-19

You Father, the creator of everything in heaven and on earth, I praise your Holy name! I pray that from your glorious unlimited resources you will endue me with your mighty strength through your Holy Spirit. I pray that Christ will be more and more at home in my heart as I trust in you. May my roots go down deep into the soil of your marvelous love. I pray that I may begin to comprehend, as I should, just how wide, long, high and deep is your love for me. Fill me today with all of your fullness and power, in Jesus mighty name. Amen and Amen. Father, in the Name of Jesus, open doors in my life today. Save and Set me free! Grant me a double portion of your Spirit as I take back everything that the devil has stolen~

- Emotional Health
- Physical Health
- Finances
- Relationships
- Children
- Jobs
- Homes
- My Marriage

I cancel every plot, plan and scheme the enemy has devised against us in the name of Jesus. I declare that no weapon formed against us shall prosper. I speak LIFE into every dead situation. I thank you that nothing is over until you say it's over! I speak this prophetically into our lives and into our situations~

- our households are blessed
- our health is blessed
- our marriage is blessed
- our finances are blessed
- our jobs are blessed
- our parents are blessed
- our siblings are blessed
- our children are blessed
- our grandchildren are blessed
- our ministries are blessed
- our decisions are blessed
- our friends are blessed
- our church is blessed
- our neighbors are blessed
- our hearts and minds are open to your will

May all this be according to your perfect will and plan for our lives, in Jesus name, Amen.

L.A. Mars January 2011

Wisdom ~ Anger ~ Foolishness

I will extol you O LORD, for you have lifted me up and not let my enemies rejoice over me. O LORD my God, I cried to you for help and you healed me. O LORD, you have brought up my soul from Sheol. You have kept me alive that I would not go down to the pit. Sing praise to the LORD, you his godly ones and give thanks to his holy name. For his anger is but for a moment, his favor is for a lifetime, weeping may last for a night but a shout of joy comes in the morning. Psalm 30:1-5

The fear of the LORD is the beginning of knowledge, fools despise wisdom and instruction. Proverbs 1:7

Hatred stirs up strife, but love covers all transgressions. Proverbs 10:12

When there are many words, transgression is unavoidable, but he who restrains his lips is wise. Proverbs 10:19

The tongue of the righteous is as choice silver, the heart of the wicked is worth little. Proverbs 10:20

The lips of the righteous feed many, but fools die for lack of understanding. Proverbs 10:21

The mouth of the righteous flows with wisdom, but the perverted tongue will be cut out. Proverbs 10:31

The lips of the righteous bring forth what is acceptable, but the mouth of the wicked what is perverted. Proverbs 10:32

When pride comes, then dishonor, but with the humble, wisdom. Proverbs 11:2

But a man of understanding keeps silent. Proverbs 11:12b

An evil man is ensnared by the transgression of his lips.
Proverbs 12:13a

A man will be satisfied with good by the fruit of his words.
Proverbs 12:14a

There is one who speaks rashly like the thrusts of a sword, but the tongue of the wise brings healing. Proverbs 12:18

From the fruit of a man's mouth he enjoys good. Proverbs 13:2a

The one who guards his mouth preserves his life, the one who opens wide his lips comes to ruin. Proverbs 13:3

Leave the presence of a fool, or you will not discern words of knowledge. Proverbs 14:7

A quick-tempered man acts foolishly. Proverbs 14:17a

He who is slow to anger has great understanding, but he who is quick-tempered exacts folly. Proverbs 14:29

A gentle answer turns away wrath, but a harsh word stirs up anger.
Proverbs 15:1

A soothing tongue is a tree of life, but perversion in it crushes the spirit. Proverbs 15:4

The lips of the wise spread knowledge, but the hearts of fools are not so. Proverbs 15:7

A hot-tempered man stirs up strife, but the slow to anger calms a dispute. Proverbs 15:18

A man has joy in an apt answer, and how delightful is a timely word.
Proverbs 15:23

Pleasant words are pure. Proverbs 15:26b

The heart of the righteous ponders how to answer, but the mouth of the wicked pours out evil things. Proverbs 15:28

Righteous lips are the delight of kings and he who speaks right is loved. Proverbs 16:13

The wise in heart will be called understanding and sweetness of speech increases persuasive-ness. Proverbs 16:21

The heart of the wise instructs his mouth and adds persuasive-ness to his lips. Proverbs 16:23

Pleasant words are a honeycomb, sweet to the soul and healing to the bones. Proverbs 16:24

He who is slow to anger is better than the mighty. Proverbs 16:32a

He who restrains his words has knowledge, and he who has a cool spirit is a man of understanding. Proverbs 17:27

Even a fool, when he keeps silent, is considered wise; when he closes his lips, he is considered prudent. Proverbs 17:28

The words of a man's mouth are deep waters. Proverbs 18:4a

A fool's lips bring strife, and his mouth calls for blows. Proverbs 18:6

A fool's mouth is his ruin, and his lips are the snare of his soul. Proverbs 18:7

The words of a whisperer are like dainty morsels, and they go down into the innermost parts of the body. Proverbs 18:8

He who gives an answer before he hears, it is folly and shame to him. Proverbs 18:13

With the fruit of a man's mouth his stomach will be satisfied, he will be satisfied with the product of his lips. Proverbs 18:20

Death and life are in the power of the tongue and those who love it will eat its fruit. Proverbs 18:21

A man's discretion makes him slow to anger and it is his glory to overlook a transgression. Proverbs 19:11

Keeping away from strife is an honor for a man, but any fool will quarrel. Proverbs 20:3

There is gold and an abundance of jewels, but the lips of knowledge are a more precious thing. Proverbs 20:15

He who guards his mouth and his tongue, guards his soul from troubles. Proverbs 21:23

Do not associate with a man given to anger or go with a hot-tempered man, or you will learn his ways and find a snare for yourself. Proverbs 22:24-25

An honest answer is like a kiss on the lips. Proverbs 24:26

Do not go out hastily to argue your case, otherwise what will you do in the end when your neighbor humiliates you? Proverbs 25:8

Like apples of gold in settings of silver is a word spoken in right circumstances. Proverbs 25:11

Like an earring of gold and an ornament of fine gold is a wise reprover to a listening ear. Proverbs 25:12

By forbearance a ruler may be persuaded and a soft tongue breaks the bone. Proverbs 25:15

Like a dog returns to its vomit is a fool who repeats his folly. Proverbs 26:11

As in water face reflects face, so the heart of man reflects man. Proverbs 27:19

He who conceals his transgressions will not prosper, but he who confesses and forsakes them will find compassion. Proverbs 28:13

Scorners set a city aflame, but wise men turn away anger. Proverbs 29:8

A fool always loses his temper, but a wise man holds it back. Proverbs 29:11

Do you see a man who is hasty in his words? There is more hope for a fool than for him. Proverbs 29:20

An angry man stirs up strife, and a hot- tempered man abounds in transgression. Proverbs 29:22

Do not be eager in your heart to be angry, for anger resides in the bosom of fools. Ecclesiastes 6:9

You have heard that the ancients were told, 'You shall not commit murder' and 'Whoever commits murder shall be liable to the court.' But I say to you that everyone who is angry with his brother shall be guilty before the court and whoever says to his brother, 'You good-for nothing,' shall be guilty before the supreme court and whoever says, 'You fool," shall be guilty enough to go into the fiery hell. Matthew 5:22

Be angry and yet do not sin, do not let the sun go down on your anger. Ephesians 4:26

But now you also, put them all aside; anger, wrath, malice, slander and abusive speech from your mouth. Colossians 3:8

Husbands, love your wives and do not be embittered against them. Colossians 3:19

Fathers, do not exasperate your children, so that they will not lose heart. Colossians 3:21

This you know, my beloved brethren. But everyone must be quick to hear, slow to speak and slow to anger, for the anger of man does not achieve the righteousness of God. James 1:19-20

Never take your own revenge beloved, but leave room for the wrath of God, for it is written, "Vengeance is mine, I will repay," says the LORD. Romans 12:19

The LORD is slow to anger and great in power. Nahum 1:3a

angry - H. 3707, ka'as- to be angry, be vexed, be incensed, to anger, provoke, to provoke to anger. Also see H. 3708, ka'as'- general uneasiness and anxiety, inwardly focused, anguish, grief, focused toward an object: anger resentment. ~

angry - G. 3710 orgizo- be angry, enraged, to feel and express strong displeasure and hostility; this can range from petty human anger to the righteous anger of God toward sinful disobedience. ~

wrath - The emotional response to perceived wrong and injustice, often translated anger, indignation, vexation and irritation. ~

Holman Dictionary

anger - The English rendering of at least ten biblical words, of which the most common is Hebrew 'aph, which could also mean "snorting."

The Old Testament condemns anger because it encourages folly and evil and because vengeance belongs to the God.

Elsewhere it calls for restraint from those confronted by anger. In the New Testament, anger is among those emotions that provoke God's wrath and is regarded as alien to godliness. There is however a righteous anger as when Jesus condemned the misuse of the temple, the corruption of children and a lack of compassion. ~ Zondervan Bible Dictionary

anger - a strong feeling of displeasure and usually of antagonism, rage.   Webster's Dictionary

Synonyms ~ anger, ire, rage, fury, indignation, wrath

L.A. Mars October 2010

I AM ~ I AM

I am united with the Lord and one with him in Spirit -
1 Corinthians 6:17
I am complete in Christ - Colossians 2:10
I am assured that all things work together for good - Romans 8:28
I am chosen and appointed to bear fruit - John 15:16
I am a minister of reconciliation - 2 Corinthians 5:18
I am God's co-worker - 2 Corinthians 6:1
I am throwing off everything that hinders - Hebrews 12:1b
I am sanctified through and through, so my whole spirit, soul
and body will be blameless at his coming - 1 Thessalonians 5:23
I am encouraging others and building them up - 1 Thessalonians 5:11
I am set apart for the gospel of God - Romans 1:1
I am living by faith - Romans 1:17
I am taking every thought captive and making it
obedient to Christ - 2 Corinthians 10:5
I am upheld by his righteous right hand - Isaiah 41:10
I am set free by the truth - John 8:32
I am running with endurance the race set before me - Hebrews 12:16
I am humbling myself under God's mighty hand so
he will lift me up in due time - 1 Peter 5:6
I am casting all my anxiety on him because
he cares for me - 1 Peter 5:7
I am self-controlled and alert because my enemy
is looking to devour me - 1 Peter 5:8
I am resisting him (Satan) and standing firm in the faith - 1 Peter 5:9a
I am made strong, firm and steadfast - 1 Peter 5:10a
I am hidden in the shadow of his hand - Isaiah 49:2b
I am dwelling in the shelter of the Most high - Psalm 91:1a
I am resting in the shadow of the Almighty - Psalm 91:1b
I am rescued and protected because I love and
acknowledge the LORD - Psalm 91:14
I am eager to do what is good - Titus 2:14b
I am saying no to all ungodliness and worldly passions - Titus 2:12a
I am living a self-controlled, upright and godly life while I wait
for the blessed hope - Titus 2:12b

I am the wife of the Lamb - Revelation 21:9
I am light in the LORD - Ephesians 5:8
I am trusting in the LORD and kept safe - Proverbs 29:25
I am trusting in the LORD with all my heart - Proverb 3:5

L.A. Mars June 2008

It was in the summer of 2008 I put these verses together and began using them in my daily devotions so that I'd get a grasp on just how precious I really am in Christ. I wanted and needed to "know" who I was so that when the enemy came in like a flood, I would not be overcome by the lies he was whispering into my ears. God's word is alive and active to the pulling down of strongholds! Hallelujah!

Try it, you'll like it!

I AM ~ I AM ~ I AM

I am created in my Father's image ~ Genesis 1:26
I am my Father's treasured possession ~ Deuteronomy 14:2
I am the apple of my Father's eye ~ Zechariah 2:8
I am fearfully and wonderfully made ~ Psalm 139:14
I am precious in my Father's sight ~ Isaiah 43:4a
I am a crown of beauty in the hand of my Father ~ Isaiah 62:3
I am loved so much my Father has counted the
hairs on my head ~ Matthew 10:30
I am united with my Father and one with
him in Spirit ~ 1 Corinthians 6:17
I am supplied with all I need according to my Father's
riches in glory ~ Philippians 4:19
I am my Father's workmanship ~ Ephesians 2:10
I am complete in him ~ Colossians 2:10
I am approved by my Father ~ 1 Thessalonians 2:4a
I am given everything I need for life & godliness through my
knowledge of Jesus, my Father's Son ~ 2 Peter 1:3
I am a child of God and my Father loves me ~ 1 John 3:1
I am filled with my Father's Spirit ~ 1 John 4:13

I am trusting my Father with all my heart
I am hidden in the shadow of my Father's hand
I am hemmed in by my Father
I am never left or forsaken
I am resting in the shadow of the Almighty, my Father
I am dwelling in the shelter of the Most High, my Father
I am rescued and protected by my Father
I am crowned with love and compassion by my Father
I am a gift to Jesus from my Father

L.A. Mars September 2008

My Daily Bread
To you O LORD I lift up my soul. Psalm 25:1

Our Father who art in heaven, hallowed be thy name. Thy Kingdom come, thy will be done, on earth as *it is* in heaven. Give us this day our daily bread, forgive us our trespasses as we forgive those who trespass against us. Lead us not into temptation but deliver us from evil, for thine is the kingdom and the power and the glory, forever and ever, Amen. Matthew 6:9-13

Praise the LORD, O my soul, all my inmost being, praise his holy name! Praise the LORD, O my soul, and forget not all his benefits-who forgives all our sins and heals all our diseases. Psalm 103:1-3

Surely he took up our infirmities and carried our sorrows, yet we considered him stricken by God, smitten by him and afflicted. But he was pierced for our iniquities, the punishment that brought us peace was upon him and by his wounds we are healed. Isaiah 53:4-5

He took up our infirmities and carried our diseases. Matthew 8:17b

He himself bore our sins in his body on the tree, so that we might die to sins and live for righteousness, by his wounds you have been healed. 1 Peter 2:24

He heals the brokenhearted and binds up their wounds. Psalm 147:3

He sent forth his word and healed them, he rescued them from the grave. Psalm 107:20

I have heard your prayer and seen your tears, I will heal you. 2 Kings 20:5b

O LORD my GOD, I called to you for help and you healed me. Psalm 30:2

But I will restore you to health and heal your wounds, declares the LORD. Jeremiah 30:17a

Worship the LORD your God and his blessing will be on your food and water. I will take away sickness from among you. Exodus 23:25

And the prayer offered in faith will make the sick person well, the Lord will raise him up. James 5:15a

I will not die but live and will proclaim what the LORD has done. Psalm 118:17

But for you who revere my name, the sun of righteousness will rise with healing in its wings. And you will go out and leap like calves released from the stall. Malachi 4:2

Do not be wise in your own eyes, fear the LORD and shun evil. This will bring health to your body and nourishment to your bones. Proverbs 3:7-8

My son, pay attention to what I say, listen closely to my words. Do not let them out of your sight; keep them within your heart, for they are life to those who find them and health to a mans whole body. Proverbs 4:20-22

The LORD will keep you free from every disease. Deuteronomy 7:15a

So tell them, "as surely as I live, declares the LORD, I will do to you the very things I heard you say". Numbers 14:28

... I tell you the truth, if you have faith as small as a mustard seed, you can say to this mountain, 'move from here to there' and it will move. Nothing will be impossible for you. Matthew 17:20b

No weapon forged against you will prevail, and you will refute every tongue that accuses you. This is the heritage of the servants of the

LORD and this is their vindication from me, declares the LORD. Isaiah 54:17

...so is my word that goes out from my mouth, it will not return to me empty, but will accomplish what I desire and achieve the purpose for which I sent it. Isaiah 55:11

...the God who gives life to the dead and calls things that are not as though they were. Romans 4:17b

For we are God's workmanship, created in Christ Jesus to do good works, which God prepared in advance for us to do. Ephesians 2:10

And my God will meet all your needs according to his glorious riches in Christ Jesus. Philippians 4:19

For he has rescued us from the dominion of darkness and brought us into the kingdom of the Son he loves, in whom we have redemption, the forgiveness of sins. Colossians 1:13-14

You dear children, are from God and have overcome them, because the one who is in you is greater than the one who is in the world. 1 John 4:4

Dear friend, I pray that you may enjoy good health and that all may go well with you, even as your soul is getting along well. 3 John 2

The LORD will grant that the enemies who rise up against you will be defeated before you. They will come at you from one direction but flee from you in seven. Deuteronomy 28:7

Go into all the world and preach the good news to all creation. Whoever believes and is baptized will be saved, but whoever does not believe will be condemned. And these signs will accompany those who believe. In my name they will drive out demons, they will speak in new tongues, they will pick up snakes with their hands and when they drink deadly poison, it will not hurt them at all, they will place their hands on sick people and they will get well. Mark 16:15-18

I have given you authority to trample on snakes and scorpions and to overcome all the power of the enemy, nothing will harm you. Luke 10:19

The Spirit of the Lord is on me, because he has anointed me to preach the good news to the poor. He has sent me to proclaim freedom for the prisoners and recovery of sight to the blind, to release the oppressed, to proclaim the year of the Lord's favor. Luke 4:18-19

As you go, preach this message "The kingdom of heaven is near. Heal the sick, raise the dead, cleanse those who have leprosy and drive out demons. Freely you have received, freely give." Matthew 10:7

The Lord will rescue me from every evil attack and will bring me safely to his heavenly kingdom. To him be glory forever and ever. Amen! 2 Timothy 4:18

They overcame him by the blood of the Lamb and by the word of their testimony. Revelation 12:11a

But seek first his kingdom and his righteousness, and all these things will be given to you as well. Matthew 6:33

The weapons we fight with are not the weapons of the world. On the contrary, they have divine power to demolish strongholds. We demolish arguments and every pretension that sets itself up against the knowledge of God, and we take captive every thought to make it obedient to Christ. 2 Corinthians 10:4-5

The thief comes only to steal kill and destroy, I have come that they may have life and have it to the full. John 10:10

For everyone who asks receives, he who seeks finds and to him who knocks, the door will be opened. Luke 11:10

I tell you the truth, anyone who has faith in me will do what I have been doing. He will do even greater things than these, because I am going to the Father. John 14:12-14

If you remain in me and my words remain in you, ask whatever you wish, and it will be given you. John 15:7

The Spirit gives life, the flesh counts for nothing. The words I have spoken to you are spirit and they are life. John 6:63

A cheerful heart is good medicine, but a crushed spirit dries up the bones. Proverbs 17:22

The fear of the LORD adds length to life, but the years of the wicked are cut short. Proverbs 10:27

Reckless words pierce like a sword, but the tongue of the wise brings healing. Proverbs 12:18

The tongue that brings healing is a tree of life, but a deceitful tongue crushes the spirit. Proverbs 15:4

Commit to the LORD whatever you do and your plans will succeed. Proverbs 16:3

The Lord is my Shepherd, I shall not be in want. Psalm 23:1

Praise be to the Lord, our God and Savior, who daily bears our burdens. Psalm 68:19

Blessed are all who fear the LORD, who walk in his ways. You will eat the fruit of your labor, blessings and prosperity will be yours. Psalm 128:1-2

The LORD is my rock, my fortress and my deliverer; my God is my rock, in whom I take refuge. I call to the LORD, who is worthy of praise and I am saved from my enemies. Psalm 18:2a-3

Cast your cares on the LORD and he will sustain you. Psalm 55:22a

I can do *all things* through Christ who strengthens me.
Philippians 4:13

So do not fear, for I am with you, do not be dismayed, for I am your God. I will strengthen you and help you, I will uphold you with my righteous right hand. Isaiah 41:10

The tongue has the power of life and death, and those who love it will eat its fruit. Proverbs 18:21

For the LORD God is a sun and a shield, the LORD bestows favor and honor, no good thing does he withhold from those whose walk is blameless. Psalm 84:11

Come near to God and he will come near to you. James 4:8a

Now may the Lord's strength be displayed, just as you have declared. Numbers 14:17

Jesus answered, it is written: *'man does not live on bread alone, but on every word that comes from the mouth of God.'* Matthew 4:4

To the man who pleases him, God gives wisdom, knowledge and happiness... Ecclesiastes 2:26a

"For I know the plans I have for you, declares the LORD, plans to prosper you and not harm you, plans to give you a hope and a future." Then you will call upon me and come and pray to me, and I will listen to you. You will seek me and find me when you seek me with all your heart. Jeremiah 29:11-13

Let us then approach the throne of grace with confidence, so that we may receive mercy and find grace to help us in our time of need. Hebrews 4:16

Cast your bread upon the waters, for after many days you will find it again. Ecclesiastes 11:1

... the prince of this world now stands condemned. John 16:11b

Take heart! I have overcome the world. John 16:33

"Never will I leave you, never will I forsake you." Hebrews 13:5b

Jesus Christ is the same yesterday and today and forever. Hebrews 13:8

Praise be to the God and Father of our Lord Jesus Christ, who has blessed us in the heavenly realms with every spiritual blessing in Christ. Ephesians 1:3

Therefore God exalted to the highest place and gave him the name that is above every name, that at the name of Jesus every knee should bow, in heaven and on earth and under the earth. Philippians 2:9-10

The LORD is my Shepherd, I shall not want. He makes me to lie down in green pastures, he leads me beside the still waters. He restores my soul. He guides me in paths of righteousness for his name's sake. Yea, though I walk through the valley of the shadow of death, I will fear no evil, for you are with me, thy rod and thy staff, they comfort me. He prepares a table before me in the presence of mine enemies, he anoints my head with oil and my cup overflows. Surely goodness and mercy shall follow me all the days of my life and I will dwell in the house of the LORD for ever. Psalm 23:1-6

It is of the LORD'S mercies that we are not consumed, because his compassions fail not. *They are* new every morning~ great *is* thy faithfulness. The LORD *is* my portion saith my soul, therefore will I hope in him. Lamentations 3:22-24

Let nothing move you. Always give yourselves fully to the work of

the Lord, because you know that your labor is not in vain.
1 Corinthians 15:58b

Your word, O LORD, is eternal~ it stands firm in the heavens.
Psalm 119:89

Trust in the LORD with all your heart and lean not on your own understanding; in all your ways acknowledge him, and he will make your paths straight. Proverbs 3:5

"It's not by might nor by power, but by my Spirit" says the Lord Almighty. Zechariah 4:6b

I pray also that the eyes of your heart may be enlightened in order that you may know the hope to which he has called you, the riches of his glorious inheritance in the saints, and his incomparably great power for us who believe. That power is like the working of his mighty strength, which he exerted in Christ when he raised him from the dead and seated him at his right hand in the heavenly realms.
Ephesians 1:18-20

L.A. Mars September 2008

Don't assume that you know it all. Run to God! Run from evil!
Message Bible

Don't be impressed with your own wisdom.
Instead, fear the LORD and turn away from evil. NLT

Never let yourself think that you are wiser than you are, simply obey the Lord and refuse to do wrong. Good News Translation

Stop trying to figure everything out on your own and
TRUST GOD!
Proverbs 3:5

Testimonies from Greater Works Ministry School

2004-2008

"My shoulders were 'frozen' for more than five years. To raise my arms would cause severe pain, but with prayer and laying on of hands, my shoulders were healed within minutes. I was diagnosed with carpal tunnel in my left hand. When my hand was touched and prayed over, Jesus healed my hand completely. It has been over three years now and I am still saying 'Thank you Jesus!'" - *DEB JAAKOLA, 53 MOUNDSVIEW, MN*

"I have lived with headaches and migraines all my life. Emotionally spent from the discord in my life, I was under a physician's care for depression, ADD, anxiety and panic attacks. I was invited to Greater Works Ministries Healing School and with some reluctance I went. Each week I went forward for ministry. The headaches and migraines are gone! My mind and soul are renewed, refreshed and clear. The anger, frustration and resentment are gone. Love and a sense of peace fill my heart. I am no longer running from doctor to doctor for answers or drugs to alleviate the pain- there is none! Thank you Jesus, praise God!" - PAMELA PETERSON, 54, MAPLE GROVE, MN

"I was invited to one of the first classes of Greater Works Ministries in 2005. I was curious and also longing for healing in my knees and hip. I had very much difficulty kneeling for prayer. During our study, when they laid hands on me, God touched me and performed the healing of my knees and hip. Thank you Jesus for the precious time I can kneel and give you praise." - LIL LUKEN, 82, SPRING LAKE PARK, MN JUNE 2005

"I had pain in the joints of my fingers and was prone to flare ups with increased use of my fingers, sometimes lasting for days. It has been increasing for about two years. Since prayer, I have not experienced the pain in my joints as before. Praise God! I can snap my fingers without pain. When I get a twinge of pain in my fingers, I rebuke it in Jesus' name and plead healing through Jesus' blood and thank Jesus. It sometimes takes 2 or 3 times, but from that day to this it leaves!"
- *Debbie, Summer 2008*

"God is so awesome! This morning a staff member came up to me and said his back hurts. I just automatically said, "Do you want me to pray for you?" He said, "Yes." There were 3-4 aides by him that said, "She prays for healing." Word spreads. Anyways, I told him to stop by when he gets time. I really didn't think he was going to. He came in and I prayed for his hands that had a 1 inch difference and his legs that also had a 1 inch difference. When we got done, he had no more back pain and his arms and legs were the same. I hope that boosted his faith in God. He was amazed. He goes "I believe." The people around us as we prayed were even amazed. You get all the glory Father!" *Julie J., Plymouth MN December 2007*

"Regarding class, that was quite an experience. I don't think I have been knocked down twice in such a short time since boxing class long ago. My eyes feel very good. I have claimed the healing in Jesus' name and want it to be a faith builder for others in the class and those around me. I want God's glory to be seen through me." *Pat D., Maple Grove April 2008*

"I ministered to one of my co-workers today, it was very refreshing. I did the whole TTT. She was very receptive. She said she felt relaxed afterwards." FELISHA, ST. LOUIS PARK, MN APRIL 2008

"My left hip and pelvis have shifted forward for years causing many years of back pain. My right leg track shifted and my knee was in a compromised position causing the meniscus to tear. Despite arthroscopic surgery and seeing a Physical Therapist to learn exercises, I still have a lot of days when the pelvis is pinching again and I experience pain in my right knee. During prayer I immediately felt my hip and pelvis shifting back and no pain in my knee. I went to bed that night praising Jesus. I slept solid all night with no tossing. Normally, I had a lot of inflammation in my left hip and would have to turn a lot at night. This blessing lasted 3 days. When it returned, I would pray again and it would leave. This has become a daily exercise, sometimes five or six times a day. I've also begun to bind and rebuke this infirmity, sometimes with great relief. Other times it's very persistent. I'm standing on faith in Jesus for healing to be complete. Alleluia!" *Anonymous~ Praise you Jesus!*

"I was experiencing a lot of emotional anxiety and was very stressed when I came to class. I had an intense headache and a rebellious type of attitude which is not normal for me. It was as if I was under some kind of attack spiritually and pressed in on all sides. It was very difficult to focus. That night after being prayed over and slain in the spirit, my headache was instantly healed, all anxiety gone and total peace came over me like a soft warm blanket of love from God. Thank-you Jesus. I also have more desire and boldness to reach out to people in prayer." *Rose Ann K. of South St. Paul, MN April, 2008*

"I was feeling tingling in my muscles. When I came home from work it was there. I was prayed for and that uncomfortable feeling left my body." HANNAH D. OF ST. LOUIS PARK, MN APRIL 24, 2008

"I have no more migraine headaches since being prayed for. I have been healed of that. I also received healing in my legs when they did the "leg thing". Legs were grown out." RACHEL O., 27 OF BUFFALO, MN APRIL 12, 2007

"I suffered for three months with stomach and bowel infection, pain and gurgling in stomach, no medication helped. Jesus' spirit healed me, and continues to heal me. The healing, physical, emotional and spiritual began that night. The healing continues today four days later. I do not have any pain nor gurgling in my stomach or bowels. 'Thank you Jesus.' I also feel washed, inside and out - clean." *Ruth Teschendorf, 64 of Ingram, Texas June 14, 2007* (This is my Mom, God not only healed her body that night, he also saved her. I have had the privilege of mentoring her and watching the Lord work in her life from that day to this! Hallelujah, my God Saves!) (My Mom moved in with Jesus shortly before this publication)

"I had a heart attack eight months ago and since being prayed for my heart is good and normal. I have had no medication for four months." *Les J., 54 of Columbia Heights, MN June 21, 2007*

"For fifteen years I suffered with a stiff neck, (it felt like my head was not aligned with my spine). During the laying on of hands there was immediate relief – symptoms have not returned at all." BONNIE H. OF MAPLE GROVE, MN MAY 24, 2007

"I have suffered with back pain since 1981. I already feel a big change in my body. No more headaches and my sinus is much better each day. WOW God is awesome and I can't wait to see his power working throughout this year. I thank God for the awesome teaching from the class. I was able to do TTT on my son Sunday morning and he did an awesome praise dance at church and all were blessed. We knew that the enemy was trying to attack his body but as always, he lost again." *Vera M. of Crystal, MN May 24, 2007*

"For years I've struggled with thought disorder, anxiety and post traumatic stress disorder. Since my healing I haven't had an anxiety attacks, no voices, no paranoid thoughts or delusions. My mind is calm and clear, I have energy, I feel strong in everything I do and my relationship with God is so much better. Thank you Jesus!" SARAH J. OF BLAINE, MN APRIL 12, 2007

"Though I suffered for years with these symptoms, I was diagnosed six years ago with high blood pressure, migraine headaches, sinus and allergy problems, shortness of breath and hurting/pain in my feet. Through the laying on of hands at the Healing School I received physical healing of my body, emotional healing from depression and the devil tricking my mind, spiritual progress by feeling the Spirit of God a lot more. I had problems with my mind, body and spirit and they all changed for the best. To God be the glory. Hallelujah. Thank you Jesus." *Velma T. of S. Minneapolis, MN March 27, 2006*

"Many thanks for baptizing me with the Holy Spirit the very first session of the Healing School. I learned so much through their knowledge of scripture and the lives that they live. I believed in miracles before I attended the healing schools, but I believe in them a lot more now. In fact, I expect them. God is so very awesome and he has really changed me. Before when someone told me of problems they were facing I would pray for them when I was in the quiet of my home, or walking or driving by myself. Now, after someone tells me of a need, I hear the Holy Spirit say "Pray for them now." No one has turned me down- whether in McDonalds, at church, over the phone, wherever. Thanks be to God and to Jesus Christ our Lord and Savior, test results have come back negative, an orthopedic surgeon reported to a friend that he had never seen a hip replacement surgery heal as quickly as hers, I have seen frazzled nerves calmed and pain eased. The old hymn "What a friend we have in Jesus" comes to my mind. How true! How true! Thanks be to God for always being with us. Thank you again, Linda and Lisa. May God richly bless "you and yours" at this holiday time- and always." PEGGY A., 74 OF BROOKLYN CENTER, MN DECEMBER 2005

"Yesterday a friend of mine called and asked if I would visit a friend of hers who was at North Memorial Medical Center after having an aneurysm in her brain. I agreed and started to pray immediately for the Holy Spirit's leading. The doctors would have gone in from her groin and placed a small slinky like device in there to fill in the rupture and hope that the clots formed would not break loose and be fatal. Though her husband was skeptical and unbelieving, my friend's friend was most receptive. At one time in her life she had confessed Christ, but now felt her faith was as small as a mustard seed. I asked her what she wanted from Jesus. She responded "reassurance of the after life". I shared some scriptures from the book of John and we then prayed to renew that commitment to Christ. Her immediate response was, "I feel different". I went on to share the whole Gospel message, that not only did Jesus die for our sins, but that He also took our sicknesses and diseases on the cross too. He did that so that we don't need to carry them! My new friend agreed, and we spoke new arteries into her body and rebuked any infections. I prayed for her then I left her in God's hands. When the Surgeon came in this morning he wanted to redo the angiogram to see for himself what was going on. He found *NOTHING!* There were no signs of an aneurysm at all! God created us and He can recreate us. That is exactly what he did with Julie's veins! Hallelujah, hallelujah, hallelujah!!! He is our Healer... He is our Healer! Praise him with me all of you for his faithfulness, God's Word works!" *Lisa Mars, 45 of Blaine, MN*

(This is one of my own testimonies! Hallelujah!)

"Praise the Lord! Satan is defeated big time at the cross. I forgot to mention to you that I put my hands on my son after class. He had had a bad cough before that. Now he is healed. Thanks to our Lord! Hallelujah!" *Christa L. of NE Minneapolis, MN APRIL 7, 2007*

"I thought I knew much about healing, until I went through Greater Works Healing School. I not only learned the healing scriptures, I witnessed and experienced the deliverance of many things. I myself experienced two significant healings, one of watching my diabetes sugar levels come into balance, I now only need my insulin at night vs. with every meal. The second healing I received is about my body being afflicted with Cystic Fibrosis, which is on its way to a full manifestation of healing. I had a lung infection called cepacia, during the weeks of healing school. I watched this go from the highest level of a four down to a wonderful level one. God's healing power is available to us all, the authority is given to us, and I have learned I only need to exercise my faith." *Kelly S. 38, NE Minneapolis. MN*

1st National Day of Healing Testimonies

2006

"I came by the church on Saturday. I had had the opportunity to be prayed for by Greater Works Ministries students. Besides praying to have my blood pressure reduced (I will be writing back to give a praise report), they also prayed for my son who has autism. Today at school, my son's teacher wrote: 'Christa, We were so happy to see the happy smiling Kenny this morning. What a difference! He is eating again as well. We will keep an eye on what he eats… we will keep it healthy and low fat so he can stay trim.' Thank you very much!!! Praise the Lord Jesus!!!" *Christa S. of Minneapolis, MN 10-30-06*

UPDATE I came to your church to reduce my blood pressure on the 1st National Day of Healing. I went to check my blood pressure after Christmas Day, Hallelujah! It was 118/87. Praise the name of Jesus, the Most High God. Thank you. *DECEMBER 27, 2006*

UPDATE Glory to God! My B.P. was around 150/110. It went down to 118/87 on December 26th. Yesterday it was 133/88. I would say that the range is much lower than three months ago. *January 4, 2007*

"Thanks to Greater Works Ministries for encouraging me to pray with greater expectation for the sick. I have been praying for all kinds of new body parts lately for patients. I decided to review the healing books for help in praying for patients. I happened to open it to the new body part chapter. It inspired me to pray in that way. Most of my prayers are in private on their behalf. A coma patient awakened after a section of their brain was removed. The family was not open to a chaplain's visit but we were praying for them. I rejoiced in my heart when I heard the patient talking. Prayer does make a difference! Thank you again for stirring up my prayer life!" JULIE S. OF SHOREVIEW, MN NOVEMBER 11, 2006

"I just wanted to let you know what a blessing it was for my family to be prayed for on Saturday! I'm truly grateful for your ministry and for everyone involved who were willing to give of their time and their gifts. I would like to especially like to thank the two women who spent so much time praying for Alex, my husband and myself. Alex says he really does feel lighter in spirit and has noticed that he is able to communicate verbally more easily. I feel the heaviness on my heart has been lifted! Praise God! I've placed the prayer cards you gave me on my bathroom mirror. Thank you for those! I found the experience to be uplifting and healing. I learned some things about myself and recognize that I have a lot more to learn! God is good!" JULIE S. OF PLYMOUTH, MN OCTOBER 30, 2006

"It is with great excitement that I will now testify to God's faithfulness and power! In three hours we ministered to 39 individuals on the 1st National Day of Healing! Ears were opened, knees were healed, backs straightened from scoliosis, arms and legs grown out and attitudes were adjusted! Many were delivered from stress, anxiety, fears, allergies, stomach pains, arthritis, memory loss, TMJ, bladder infections, blood pressure problems, carpel tunnel, cysts, hips out of joint, weight loss problems, joint pain, detoxification, osteopenia, hand eye coordination, speech problems, backs were healed so they could stand up straight and cancer was rebuked! People were ministered to mentally, emotionally and spiritually! Oh isn't our God so good!" LISA MARS OF BLAINE, MN

(Another one of my own testimonies, Hallelujah Papa God!!!)

On top of all that, three individuals accepted Christ as their personal Savior and three others were filled with the Holy Spirit *and* spoke in other tongues! Many more were simply encouraged in the Word!

As if that wasn't enough fun for us, our team of fifteen were stirred up in our own faith which encouraged us to continue ministering the love of God and the Holy Spirits healing power in our every day lives!

Thank you Jesus!

Hallelujah

Greater Works Ministries Healing Service

July 2006 in Brooklyn Park, MN

Kathy asked God to remove facial stiffness, adjust hips and remove the pain in her right knee and legs. All the pain left and her face was no longer drawn tight!

David prayed for many things in his body~ sleep apnea, appestat, back pain, dyslexia, bi-polar and tremors from the side effects of meds he used. After a prayer of repentance repeated for unforgiveness and prayer to release childhood memories keeping him bound, all back pain was gone. We followed up by giving him scriptures to encourage him until he's completely free.

Jean S. prayed for pain in her right knee and the pain left.

JoAnn, my fingernails are restored, unforgiveness and deliverance from smoking. After praying she threw out the cigarettes and lighters.

Julie testified of being healed from sleep apnea recently.

Jean F. testified to deliverance from cigarettes and her son's deaf ear being opened and another little 3 year old girl she laid hands on who was deaf~ but is no longer. This all happened after she attended the Healing School.

Because of the *LORD's* great love we are
not consumed for his compassions never fail.
They are new every morning, great is your
faithfulness. Lamentations 3:22-23

I am not ashamed of the gospel because
it is the power of *God* for the salvation of
everyone who believes. Romans 1:16

They overcame him by the blood of the
Lamb and by the word of their testimony.
Revelation12:11a

I love the song *"Standing on the Promises of God"* because it encapsulates what the premise of this book is all about. As we search for and find God's promises in his word, (hidden they are ~ yet in plain sight) they will not fail! Hallelujah! I will prevail~ they will cleanse, purify, liberate and make us free! In so doing (standing on his promises) we'll overcome daily and will with time, rest secure in his love for us. For no matter how many promises there are, they are all "Yes" and "Amen"! Amen and Amen! God is faithful to perform his word if we will just let it ring out! I have included the words to the song so that you may sing for yourself what Russell K. Carter penned in 1886. The scripture he based the song on is found in Hebrews 10:23.

Standing on the Promises of God

Standing on the promises of Christ my King
Through eternal ages let His praises ring
Glory in the highest I will shout and sing
Standing on the promises of God

Refrain~
Standing, standing
Standing on the promises of God my Savior
Standing, standing
I'm standing on the promises of God

Standing on the promises that cannot fail
When the howling storms of doubt and fear assail
By the living Word of God I shall prevail
Standing on the promises of God

Standing on the promises I now can see
Perfect, present cleansing in the blood for me
Standing in the liberty where Christ makes free

Standing on the promises of God
Standing on the promises of Christ the Lord
Bound to him eternally by loves strong cord
Overcoming daily with the Spirit's sword
Standing on the promises of God

Standing on the promises I cannot fall
List'ning every moment to the Spirit's call
Resting in my Savior as my all in all
Standing on the promises of God

Russell K. Carter ~ public domain 1886

**For no matter how many promises God has made,
they are "Yes" in Christ. So through him the "Amen"
is spoken by us to the glory of God.**
2 Corinthians 1:20

**"Now I am about to go the way of all the earth.
You know with all your heart and
soul that not one of all the good promises the
Lord your God gave you has failed.
Every promise has been fulfilled, not one has failed.**
Joshua 23:14

**Let us hold unswervingly to the hope we profess,
for he who promised is faithful.**
Hebrews 10:23

The following entry entitled "My Son" is a snapshot in time from his diagnosis on April 21, 2003 until the day he moved in with Jesus, February 11, 2004. It was a very long and a very short ten months from diagnosis to death. I trust you will come to know and love him just a bit by reading the next few pages. I thank you for allowing me to share him~ my precious son, with you!

"My Son"

Jake (as he preferred to be called) was born on March 12, 1988 at eleven minutes to eleven, just approaching the midnight hour. We gave him the name, *Jacob Gerald Mars*, his middle name given in honor of his maternal grandfather... they became good buddies in this life.

Jake was diagnosed with ALL/NK Leukemia~ April 21, 2003. I didn't even know what leukemia was, but have since gotten a full education on it and then some. Most patients with this type of leukemia wouldn't have a transplant, however, "Natural Killer" or NK cells made a transplant immediately necessary. Eighteen of the 24 cases that in the study had died within a year without a transplant...

Jake started chemo immediately (he was admitted to Children's hospital that day after we first went to see his Dad at work) upon diagnosis. He spent some time at Children's hospital under the care of Dr. Stephen Nelson, A.K.A. (also known as) the bow tie guy (he shaved his head and wore bowties).

Jake soon fell in love with his Doc and his Doc soon fell in love with Jake too. Our Doctor, Bow Tie Guy was so warm, encouraging and personable. Jake did chemo for a month and then he was to have eight days of radiation. The chemo put him into remission and despite taking meds to prevent a relapse, by the time he finished radiation the cancer had grown back. The NK cell is apparently very aggressive. So round two of chemo, this round he was inpatient for twenty-three days which put him into a better remission. (if that's possible)

It was mid July by now, about eight weeks after his diagnosis. We had a couple weeks of prep time at the University of Minnesota where his transplant would take place. Donors of stem cells were found rather quickly. There would be seven days of preparation, more chemo and total body radiation Jake submitted to before he could undergo the transplant that took place on July 30, 2013.

By the way, a bone marrow transplant is not a surgical procedure. The bone marrow is reddish in color and is infused just like blood through an IV line. In Jake's case they used a special line called a port, a semi-permanent line that was surgically placed into his chest that went directly into his heart.

Jake was in the hospital for 60 days straight this time... he was a real trooper and very brave. For what he endured to continue on with life, to me, was inhuman and unbearable. The only thing that made any of it bearable was knowing that Jesus was right there with us, he was there with us all of the time, performing miracles right and left. He never left us *and* we were not burned as we walked through the fire.

Jake had tutors at the hospital as he was a tenth grader at the time. When asked if he wanted to skip this year of school he resoundingly said NO. He loved school, learning and he had fun doing so! ☺

We were told that most patients return after a transplant with fevers of some kind~ and return we did. One of those return visits was to do a CSA toxicity test because he was having seizures at home. We got to ride in an ambulance that time, though it was very scary, we were not alone. I hope to never, ever, ever~ have to take that ride again.... ever.

Jake was scheduled to return back to school at the end of January as he was strong enough and well enough to do so. Though there were hurdles we had to jump through, God guided us through these also.

After two weeks in school Jake told me he had been coughing all day, as was he the nite before. (After a transplant coughing can be deadly, so it was cause for alert.) Jake had his tutor here that afternoon and then he asked for his favorite meal which was chicken soup. Of course I made the soup for him, (had I known it was to be his last meal, I never would have finished cooking it), which he ate ~ and promptly, threw it up ~ which mostly meant he was going back to the hospital. Sure enough, as before, Jake ended up with a fever and so very reluctantly we took one more trip...

Jake didn't want to go to the hospital because this was his brother Jesse's birthday weekend and we had tickets to the Timberwolves game, Jake knew if he went to the hospital he wouldn't be able to go with him to the game. This Friday night trip would be his ninth and final one. Off we went to Children's Hospital, they had no rooms available to admit him so we spent the night in a small room next to the lobby~ it was the longest and the darkest night of my entire life.

After the x-rays revealed that he may have contracted pneumonia, they concluded that they needed to transport him (by ambulance) to the University, however before they could transport him, very early that Saturday morning he was put on a respirator. He was sedated to keep him pain free and comfortable for the ambulance ride. Of course, this only heightened all of the emotions I was experiencing. By 6pm Saturday Jake hadn't awakened and I was exhausted from being up all day and all night and all day again..., so I went home as I kept my eyes on Jesus~ for he alone is my light~ my song and my strength!

By this time Jake and I had become accustomed to doing our morning and evening devotions and praying together. Later that Saturday night Jake woke up, but with a ventilator tube down his throat he of course was unable to talk so the nurse gave him pen and paper. The nurse called and told me Jake wanted to do devotions and pray with me.

She explained that when he beeped the phone three times, he was saying "I love you".

He of course was writing notes to the nurse so she could convey this to us. After praying with Jake and telling him we would see him in the morning after church, Jake beep, beep, beeped. By the way, I still have all the papers he was writing on in his last couple of days. Some are hardly legible but I don't mind, they are precious to me as they contain his last thoughts and words!

Jake would not have us skip church service to be with him, however, we were to come immediately afterwards. He had ordered a collapsible cowboy hat that we picked up for him that morning. Though he never got to wear it, it brought him great delight to have it.

Jake had spent some time with his Uncle John that Sunday morning while we were at church, the one question he asked his Uncle was this~ "Am I going to die?".

Jake was awake long enough so we could give him his hat, he was having a hard time with the tube down his throat, so they sedated him again. Late Sunday evening Jake regained consciousness long enough to call home for devotions I heard, "BEEP BEEP BEEP", it was the last time I would ever hear my son say, I love you! (in the natural that is)

On Monday and Tuesday some of Jakes major organs started to shut down... I prayed God would allow my Dad (Grandpa Jerry) to arrive from out of state before he took Jake so Grandpa could say goodbye... God is faithful... just a couple hours after Grandpa's arrival, Jake went into cardiac arrest... it was Wednesday February 11, 2014 at 10:49pm ~ or *eleven minutes to eleven* ~ the same exact time of day that he came into this here world. Although Jake didn't come home with me this time, I know he was ushered into his heavenly Fathers mansion that evening. No more pain, no more suffering and~ no more needles!

Despite his lack of consciousness during his last few days, I continued to and finished reading the book of Psalms to him the day he died... He sure loved when his Mama read to him!

The official cause of death, *"graft versus host disease"*. His lungs and organs were being attacked by the new bone marrow growing to quickly inside of him, his death was caused by the complications from the bone marrow transplant, they call it rejection.

Jake was an incredible young man. Before his diagnosis he was wandering away from his faith and God... what gives me a lot of peace is in knowing that God wooed him back to himself... *and* changed his heart. A few weeks before he died he visited his youth group where he told his leader that his Mom had become his best friend... just a year earlier he was despising me. He also told the kids that there was not time for messing around and that they should take the things of God seriously. I was so proud of him! The youth in his group have been shaken and shattered since his death.

We held his services a week after his death, there were over 800 in attendance, it truly was a celebration of his life! I didn't know we knew that many people, or that that many people knew Jake. (there were even total strangers who attended the service) About sixty kids from his school attended, some of which I have continued minimal contact with. Jakes doctors, nurses and some teachers were all there as well.

A few months prior Jake wanted to talk to Mrs. Munson, (his 1st grade teacher). I tried to find her but she was now retired and they were not able to give me any forwarding information on her... then a miracle happened. It's Mrs. Munson, she's walking up the aisle at Jakes wake. She sheepishly commented that I probably didn't remember her. Oh, but I did ~ I was so delighted to see her and share Jakes desire to see her to convey his gratitude for her... I still do not know how God brought her to us, but he did! O, to know him more! This was a huge blessing... she didn't sign the guest book so I couldn't even send a thank you note. God knows what a blessing she was on that particular day, I believe God shall surely give her her reward in heaven!

They say that young people are more sensitive of the spiritual world and of death approaching. I wondered if Jake knew he was going to leave us in just a few days. I've asked myself, "Did Jake know he was close to death", I don't know the answer to that question... but he made it a point to talk to those on the fringes of the family and he had asked his Uncle that Sunday morning if he was gonna die.... I certainly had that impression~ without a doubt on Monday morning the 9th of February, I knew in my heart of hearts that I would not be bringing my son home with me this time or ever.

Jake was always thinking of others. He was a remarkable young man, a remarkable Son. *I love him still ~ and always will.*

Jake passed into eternity

February 11, 2004 ~ 10:49pm

Jake was loved by many

Jake is with Jesus

I wrote the following and presented it at a Memorial Service that the U of M Hospital holds regularly for those who have lost loved ones. It has been very healing to remember him in this way!

"Jacob Gerald Mars"

My Jake~ He was a little stinker, a conniver, at times he cheated to win, he was a thief, he smoked, he'd lie to get his way, he swore and at times he was childish, demanding and he could be funny in a rude and crude way (boys, ya gotta love 'em!). Yet despite these common human failings, my Jakester, he died perfectly! So it is now that we choose to focus on the qualities that endeared him to each of us so very, very, very much. His deep compassion for others inspired many including me, very often when we prayed Jake would call out the name of another patient to be remembered as we prayed. I recall the time he asked me to make Christian (a Doc of his from out of state) a birthday cake because he had no family here~ so we became that family for him. Jake had concern for those less fortunate than himself and would go without so someone else could have.

Jake was a lover, he loved to have fun and he loved to make others laugh and smile, he was very silly and childish in his ways at times. He was amazed at learning new information, especially about animals and the history of the world. Jake loved to explore! He loved adventure ~ anywhere and with anyone. Before the transplant he had the opportunity to go canoeing & fishing, he also went up to the North

Shore with a neighbor. He traveled to Iowa with me to meet some missionaries I stayed with in Guatemala, this is where his hair started to fall out. He was looking forward to his Make-A-Wish trip to Ireland. Though we never got to go to, it warms our hearts to know he chose this destination because of his Dad's Irish heritage!

If you knew Jake, you knew he loved music! All kinds of music from Jazz to Country, Rock & Rap, the Oldies and the Blues, Classical, Acapella, Christian~ even the Spanish channel. To hear his Dad play guitar and sing gave him great joy and comfort. Jake was mindful, he thanked those around him for even the smallest amount of help.

Though his attitude of gratitude sometimes slipped ~ as for most ~ he not only cared, he cared a lot. About a week before he died, Jake came up from behind me in the kitchen where I was preparing him supper and said, as he was rubbing my back, *"Mom, I think I have been taking you for granted, thank you for taking such good care of me!"* I have treasured these words in my heart from that day to this. He was right and I appreciated his confession and thankfulness.

Jake just loved to be with people. He rarely complained during his illness or recovery, when asked how he was, he would inevitably say, *"Good, I'm good"*. Jake gained a new perspective on life in his final chapter, may we learn from his example. God not only healed Jakes body through modern medicine, I believe that the greater miracle was that God healed Jake's heart *and* brought him back into relationship with himself. *Thank you Jesus! Yay God!!!*

You see, Jake had been a wondering away from the faith and during this final season of his life he'd once again grown close to the Lord through his word and prayer. This thing called prayer, was and is the spiritual food that has and will continue to sustain us through this pain of our loss. I do not ponder or ask why, as John 9:3 says, "this happened so that the work of God might be displayed in his life".

Now, this does not mean that God caused Jake to have cancer, it only means that God has permitted it, he was aware of it and despite its ugliness, God will bring about an even greater good from it!

Jake knew this and he decided to trust God through it all, no matter what, so shall we do the same. What the enemy has meant for evil, the Lord will use for good (and he has!)!

Jake was a little big stinker at times
as we all can be, but~ he died perfectly.
Though he was barely 16,
Jake's life on earth was not
cut short on
February 11, 2004
Jake's life on earth was completed.

He went home to his Heavenly Father
and his Savior, Jesus Christ
where one day we too, will meet up with him.

Jake moved in with Jesus at the exact same
time of day that he entered this world.

March 12, 1988
10:49pm

~

February 11, 2004
eleven minutes to eleven pm

"to know him more"

Rest in Peace My Son

Just as I have confidence that though Jake is absent from his body, he is present with the Lord. How do I know this, because of the decision he made as a nine year old boy to accept and follow (however imperfect) Jesus as the Lord of his life. You too can have the same confidence Jake had as a nine year old when you decide for yourself to make Jesus the Lord of your life.

I want you to know that the Father in heaven loves you so very much that he sent his only Son~ Jesus, to die for you. He is waiting for you to say yes so that you may begin *"to know him more"* and walk into the Promised Land he long ago planned just for you. If you would like to receive Jesus as your Lord and Savior and meet me and my Jake in the clouds one day, read through the steps outlined in the following pages so you will know how to start your journey of faith.

I also want to let you know that once you make the decision to accept and follow Jesus, it's vital for you to find a church home. Doing so will enable you to get to know other believers who will assist you on your personal journey *"to know him more"*! I pray you will also begin to search out the great and precious promises in God's word, (the Bible) that has for you and your life! For when you seek him, the promise is~ *you shall surely find him*!

May God bless your journey with a richness of joy and peace that you have never known before~

Steps to Receive Jesus~

1. Understanding that Sin Separates us from God.

Since the beginning of time we have chosen to disobey God and go our own way which results in separation from God. Sin is choosing to do, say or think things that are against God's plan. Therefore we know the result of unforgiven sin, is death. However, God's gift is eternal life given to us through Jesus Christ when we choose to make him Lord of our lives. John 14:6 ~ Jesus answered, *"I am the way and the truth and the life. No one comes to the Father except through me.* Jesus is the only way to eternal life with him. (period) Sin separates.

2. Believing God Loves You!

For God so loved the world that he gave his one and only Son, so that whoever believes in him shall not perish but have eternal life. John 3:16 ~ Jesus is God's only Son. God loves you and wants you to know him so he can fill you with his peace and give you life ~ That's eternal life, like forever and ever. John 10:10b says: *"I have come that they may have life and have it to the full.* Since Gods plan for us is to have a full life ~ why not step into it right now?

3. Knowing that Jesus Died for our Sins.

Jesus is the only one who can bring us back to God. He died on a cross and rose from the grave to do just that, Jesus paid the ultimate price for our sin and because of this, we're now able be in relationship with the one who created us. **"There is only one God and mediator between God and men, the man Christ Jesus who gave himself as a ransom for all."** 1 Timothy 2:5-6 ~ Christ died once for our sins, he, an innocent man died for those of us who are guilty of sin, that's all of us. Jesus did this to bring us to God and thereby has provided the way ~ today I pray you will make the decision about whom you will choose to follow.

4. Receiving Jesus as your Lord.

We must actively choose to receive Jesus as our Savior by first admitting our sinfulness, then choosing to believe that God loves us (no matter what) and that Jesus died on the cross to pay for our sin. Once we do this, then we are ready to receive his love by welcoming and inviting him to become the Lord of our lives. **"As many as <u>received</u> him, to them he gave the right to become children of God, even to those who <u>believed</u> on his name."** John 1:12

When you choose (right now I hope) to turn your life over to Jesus, you may use the following prayer (or your own). Accept him today as your Savior and begin a relationship with him so that you can begin the journey "to know him more"! The abundant life he promises comes as you begin to follow him! When you believe and receive, the angels rejoice because another sinner has come home! Hallelujah! If your heart is undecided at this time, I encourage you to trust that if you ask the Lord to reveal himself to you, he will.

Prayer to Receive

God, I know that I'm a sinner and that my sin separates me from you. I understand and believe that Jesus died on a cross for my sins and that Jesus rose from the grave to give me an abundant life, now and forevermore. I know Jesus is the only way, will you please forgive me of my sinfulness and for going my own way? I choose to start living for you today. Please give me a thirst and a hunger for you and your word that I too may *"know you more"!* Fill me with your Holy Spirit, I pray this in Jesus' name. Amen.

If you prayed this, I WELCOME you to the family of God! The angels in heaven (and me) are rejoicing that you have come home!

In the same way, I tell you, there is rejoicing in the presence of the angels of God over one sinner who repents. Luke 15:10

Your journey has just begun and I bless it in Jesus name! Be sure to find a bible believing preaching church near you to help start you on this wonderful journey!

The poem on the next page is a beautiful depiction of our lives as we grow in the Lord. It speaks of how we need to trust him to unfold our lives, and as we do, we will see him take something ordinary and turn it into something *extraordinary*!. I am so delighted that you have chosen Jesus! Amen! Praise the Lord! Thank you Jesus!

Unfolding the Rose

It is only a tiny rosebud, a flower of God's design,
I cannot unfold the petals with these clumsy hands of mine.

The secret to unfolding flowers is not known to such as I,
God opens this flower so sweetly,
when in my hands they would fade and die.

If I cannot unfold a rosebud, this flower of God's design,
how can I think I have the wisdom to unfold this life of mine?

So, I'll trust him for his leading each moment of every day,
I'll look to him for guidance each step of my pilgrim way.

The pathway that lies before me,
only my Heavenly Father knows.

I'll trust him to unfold the moments,
just as he unfolds the rose.

Author Unknown

As we end our time together, I'd like to share with you one more precious jewel I've discovered. It's a short article that pretty much sums it up for me, so without further ado...

God is the Great "I AM"

God said unto Moses, I AM THAT I AM. Exodus 3:14-15
Two small words, three simple letters, "I AM". The Lord tells us repeatedly in his word that he is the great "I AM." I thought about that and wondered why he never added anything else to that statement. I felt like God was being so vague and most certainly leaving out all the wonderfully important details and awe inspiring adjectives that he could have used to enhance his own resume. Yet, he himself chose not to. At no better time do the words "less is more" or "simple abundance," hold more truth. The Lord's unvarnished, powerfully simplistic three letter title says more about our most awesome God than a whole novel ever could. This title assures us that not one miraculous trait defining our God could ever be left out. "I AM," says it all. The magnitude of this is ~ *is simply Amazing* ~ HE JUST IS!

I realized after I pondered this fact for a while that if the scriptures would have actually added the enormous sum of greatness that would be necessary to define those two impactful words, the Bible would have tripled or more in size. The possibilities are infinite because we simply can not list everything that God is! Those two words are profoundly meant to be followed by whatever we need them to say~

~ for whoever and whatever we need God to be at any given time. We get to continuously fill in the blanks as needed and there's no limit on how many chances we get to fill in those blanks~ we get to unceasingly call on Him! He's what we need, when we need it. He's never on vacation or asleep on the job. He's not too busy with more important things. He's never too tired, too angry, too frustrated or too overwhelmed to be whatever it is that we need. His customer service ranks the highest of all, he'll never put us on hold or let our message go to voice mail. He is faithfully always there.....

So I ask you , what do you need God to be today?

His name will be called...

Wonderful

Counselor

Mighty

God

Everlasting

Father

Prince of Peace

Isaiah 9:6

As we conclude I thank you for coming on this journey with me and thank you for allowing me to introduce you to my beloved son Jake and his story. Really, it's God's story. He deserves all the glory, just because "he" is. As I continue my journey *"to know him more"* I want to bless you on yours as well, so that you also "may *know him more"!*

The LORD bless you and keep you,
The LORD make his face to shine upon you & be gracious unto you,
The LORD lift up his countenance upon you and give you peace.
Numbers 6:24-26

I pray that the Father of glory may give you a spirit of wisdom and revelation in the knowledge of him that you might *"know him more"~* and that the eyes of your understanding may be enlightened so that you will know what is the hope of your calling. Amen and Amen!

As of this publication in 2021, seventeen years have passed since Jake moved in with Jesus. You know that a mother's heart always desires to make her children's dreams come true~ no matter what age they happen to be! And so it is, for Jakes 33rd birthday this March 12, his desire to go to Ireland has been fulfilled. My niece Abigail, Jakes cousin was able to bring some of his remains on a business trip with her! Yes, to Ireland! This Mama's heart have swelled with tears of gratitude and joy for this Make~A~Wish come true!!

Below is the e-mail she sent me. Abigail, I thank you so very much for loving so well and making Jake's wish (and mine) a reality! You are precious in his sight!

Hi Aunt Lisa,

I had a chance to make it out to the coast this weekend and spread Jake's ashes. It was a warm, sunny day so I drove out to Weaver's Point in Crosshaven, Ireland which is a small town about 30 minutes South of Cork. Crosshaven sits on the Celtic Sea which flows between South Ireland, Wales, England, and France and is a fairly windy spot.

When I went to spread the ashes, the wind was blowing pretty strong and steady from West to East so I made sure to stand out of the way, but right as I was almost finished pouring the ashes, a small gust of wind swooped up into my face momentarily and out of nowhere and I got a few ashes to the face. I definitely had a good laugh because I know that was Jake's presence there with me and it reminded me of how much of a prankster he liked to be, always messing with you for some good laughs.

I think that was his way of reaching out to make the moment happy and I'm going to take that as him saying he loved Ireland! Very well Jake, you won this round ha ha.

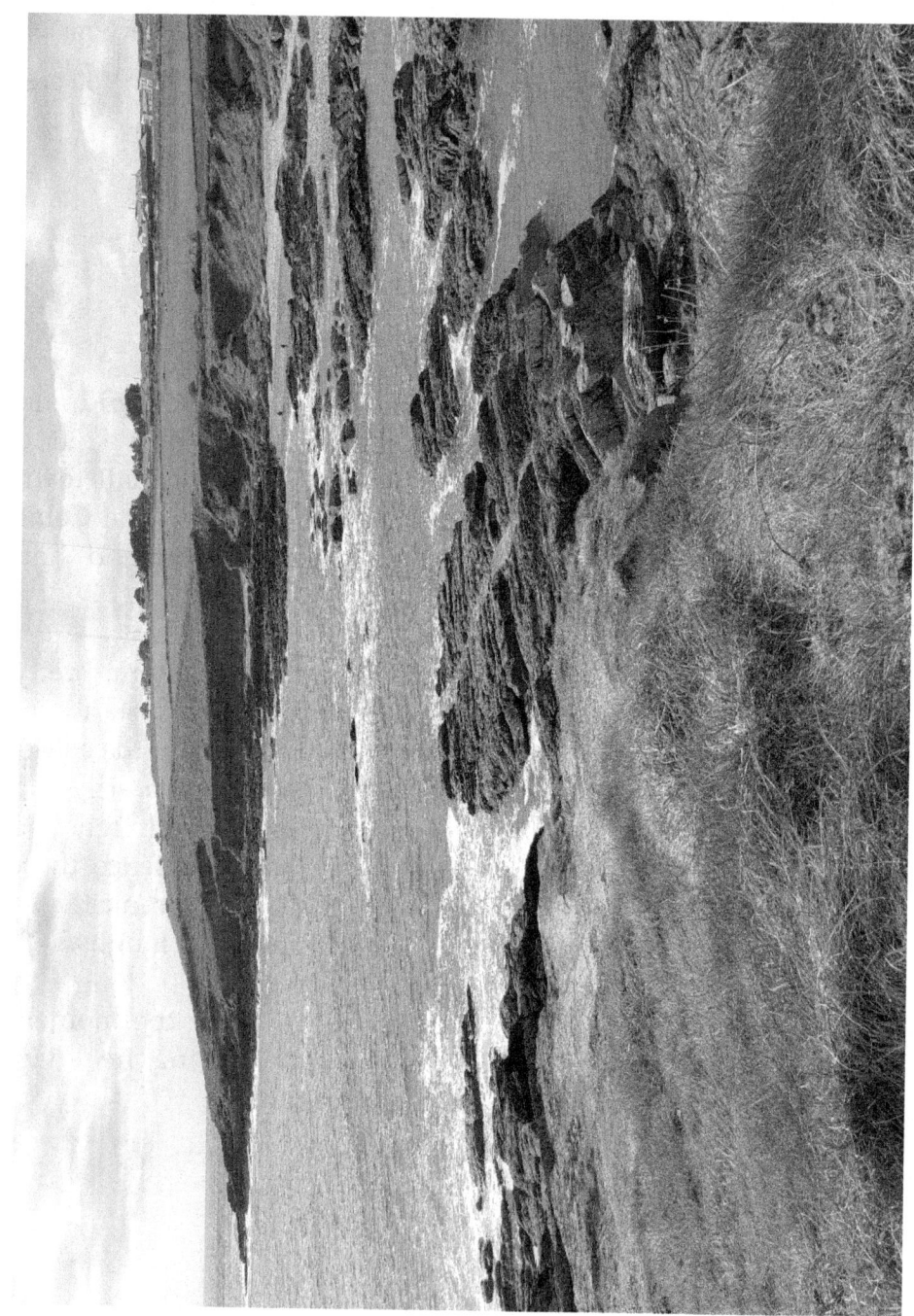

I pray that your love may abound still more and more in real knowledge and all discernment so that you may approve the things that are excellent, in order to be sincere and blameless until the day of Christ Jesus! Philippians 1:9-10

Jesus loves you and so do I!

Eternally His!

Lisa Mars

Made in the USA
Middletown, DE
27 June 2022